NEW YORK REVIEW BOOK
CLASSICS

T0253136

# THE VILLAGE OF BEN SUC

JONATHAN SCHELL (1943–2014) was born in New York
City. After majoring in Far Eastern studies at Harvard, he went
to Tokyo to study Japanese for a year. Before returning to the
United States, he stopped in Saigon, obtained a press pass, and
accompanied American soldiers who had been dispatched to
destroy the Vietnamese village of Ben Suc. His report on the
operation, an early harbinger of military and humanitarian
disaster, was published in 1967 in *The New Yorker*, where Schell
was a staff writer from 1967 to 1988. *The Fate of the Earth*,
appearing in the midst of the Reagan administration's broad
expansion of US nuclear forces, was an eloquent, widely read
essay on the perils of nuclear weapons. A senior fellow at the
Nation Institute from 1998 to 2014, as well as the peace and
disarmament correspondent for *The Nation*, Schell was also the
author of *The Abolition*, *The Gift of Time*, and *The Seventh
Decade: The New Shape of Nuclear Danger*.

WALLACE SHAWN was born in New York City and still
lives there. He is the author of several books, including *Essays*
and *Night Thoughts*, and many plays, including *The Fever*
and *The Designated Mourner*. André Gregory's productions
of *The Designated Mourner* and *Grasses of a Thousand Colors*
are available as podcasts from Gideon Media; an opera written
with Allen Shawn, *The Music Teacher*, is available from Bridge
Records. His latest play, *What We Did Before Our Moth Days*,
will eventually be seen.

# THE VILLAGE OF BEN SUC

JONATHAN SCHELL

*Introduction by*
WALLACE SHAWN

NEW YORK REVIEW BOOKS

*New York*

THIS IS A NEW YORK REVIEW BOOK
PUBLISHED BY THE NEW YORK REVIEW OF BOOKS
207 East 32nd Street, New York, NY 10016
www.nyrb.com

First published as a New York Review Books Classic in 2024.

Library of Congress Cataloging-in-Publication Data
Names: Schell, Jonathan, 1943–2014 author. | Shawn, Wallace, writer of
  introduction.
Title: The village of Ben Suc / by Jonathan Schell; introduction by Wallace
  Shawn.
Description: New York: New York Review Books, 2024. | Identifiers: LCCN
  2024001048 (print) | LCCN 2024001049 (ebook) | ISBN 9781681378497
  (paperback) | ISBN 9781681378503 (e-book)
Subjects: LCSH: Vietnam War, 1961–1975—Destruction and pillage—
  Vietnam—Bến Lức.
Classification: LCC DS557.A68 S33 2024 (print) | LCC DS557.A68 (ebook) |
  DDC 959.7/04—dc23/eng/20240119
LC record available at https://lccn.loc.gov/2024001048
LC ebook record available at https://lccn.loc.gov/2024001049

ISBN 978-1-68137-849-7
Available as an electronic book; ISBN 978-1-68137-850-3

Printed in the United States of America on acid-free paper.
10  9  8  7  6  5  4  3  2  1

# INTRODUCTION

JONATHAN SCHELL published "The Village of Ben Suc" in the July 8, 1967, issue of *The New Yorker* when he was twenty-four years old. I'd been Schell's classmate and friend since we were very young, and in 1967 I had thought we were both still more or less boys, figuring things out. When I read his article I realized that Schell had mysteriously and secretly grown up. To my amazement, he'd somehow figured out how to express his intense and passionate outlook on the world through the cool and simple sentences of a factual article about a military campaign, and I could even see his characteristic sense of the absurd glinting out from behind the grimly serious story that he told. Indeed, the essential features of his sensibility were all there in the unselfconscious pages of his first published work: a sort of tranquil respect for all living things; a steadiness of moral vision; an unblinking and almost semi-humorous awareness of the ridiculousness in what people thought and said; and, all the same, a warmth and affection that was extended even towards individuals whose actions he couldn't accept; and underlying everything else, an unmistakable kindness and gentleness of spirit. And as it turned out, his article was the beginning of his speculation on the subject to which he devoted his life: human destructiveness—the apparently unquenchable madness that drives people to kill each other—with a particular focus on the citizens of the United States.

It's quite a terrible thing to expose the crimes of one's own tribe. A deep part of our nature cries out against doing that. And the United States at that moment—1965, 1966, 1967—was not the cynical nation that it was about to become and has fully become today. On the contrary, most Americans at that moment had a very idealistic belief in the basic goodness of their country, their government, and most particularly their military establishment, which was still seen by most Americans in the glowing light of its victorious and apparently honorable role in World War Two. Schell began his career as a writer by presenting a sour, disillusioning image of the US military forces in action, and some people never forgave him for it.

Even as he was growing up, Schell had always been open to the attraction of what people called in the 1950s "different cultures." He was drawn to the ideas of Zen Buddhism when he was fifteen years old, and as he got a bit older he was inspired by his older brother, Orville, to specialize in East Asian history as an undergraduate. (Orville ultimately became one of his generation's most influential American writers and thinkers on the subject of China.) Immediately after college, Schell went to Tokyo to study Japanese, and during the year and a half he spent in Japan, the American presence in Vietnam grew from less than 100,000 soldiers to more than 300,000, and he eventually decided that on his way home to the United States he would stop off in Vietnam to see for himself what was happening there. In the early days of the war—and these were indeed the early days of the war—the American military was not particularly paranoid about what the press might write, and Schell was able to gain remarkable access to people and places using only his college newspaper's press card.

President Lyndon Johnson, as we now know, had changed his mind many times behind the scenes about whether he ought to involve the United States in a full-scale war in Vietnam. In 1965 and 1966 he decisively committed American forces to the fight. Obviously, Johnson was not an original thinker. He naturally accepted the dogmas of his time and place. And very few Americans in positions of power at that time doubted the rather elaborate theoretical framework according to which the United States was threatened in every corner of the planet by a frighteningly powerful and implacable foe, World Communism, whose clear intention was to devour the entire globe piece by piece until it finally swallowed up Washington and New York. The growing conflict between the Soviet Union and the Chinese Communists did not prevent the philosophers of American strategy from theorizing that if any country were to "fall" to Communism, Communism as a whole would grow stronger, America's will to fight it would be doubted by friends and enemies alike, and countries geographically close to the "fallen" country would fall themselves.

Vietnam had been part of the French empire. Ho Chi Minh and his Marxist-Leninist anti-colonial forces had defeated the French, but the military equation that obtained after that triumph nevertheless obliged the winning side to accept a compromise victory. Vietnam was split in half. Ho and his colleagues ruled over North Vietnam, while a strange and chaotic collection of anti-communist figures, with the United States in the background, attempted to create a nation, or the appearance of a nation, out of South Vietnam. Meanwhile Ho's revolutionary forces carried on with the struggle to achieve their ultimate goal—a unified country under their leadership—and the revolutionary guerrilla forces were indeed winning the support of the peasant population in a growing proportion of the south. This was the moment when Schell arrived in Vietnam.

Schell decided not to write in his article about Lyndon Johnson and Ho Chi Minh and whatever they might have believed or felt. He wrote exclusively about what he saw in and around a single military operation centered on a single village, the village of Ben Suc, which once had had a population of around 3,500. It turned out that Schell had a remarkable affinity for telling his tale in a quiet, deliberate, orderly manner that fit perfectly into the pages of *The New Yorker* of that era, patiently laying down one fact after another, without drawing any particular attention to himself or to what it felt like to report the story, without making any obvious attempt to attract or charm his readers or grab them by the throat, and without pandering to whatever depraved interest they might happen to have had in irrelevant but lurid material appealing to their sadistic or prurient instincts. And yet despite the calm and gentle surface of his prose and the grace and lucidity of his sentences, the story he told his readers in "The Village of Ben Suc" was shocking and grotesque. Ben Suc was in an area dominated, or possibly dominated, by the revolutionary guerrilla forces. The Americans understandably saw everyone who lived in the area as a possible threat, but there were no reliable techniques available to the American soldiers for distinguishing those in the area who might be trying to kill them from those who simply happened to live there. It was rumored and believed that the enemy guerrillas wore black clothing. That was often true, but it was also the typical clothing of a great number of Vietnamese peasants.

The American operation in Ben Suc killed perhaps twenty-five people, maybe several more, it was very hard to say. But in any case, apart from those who died, all the people currently living in Ben Suc—they were mostly women, children, and the elderly, because the men were mostly fighting in the war—were forced out of their homes by the Americans, forced off their land, and forced to leave behind every method by which they had survived, not to mention all their habitual routines and local pleasures, and then the American soldiers had drenched the grass roofs of their houses with gas and lit them on fire, and then they bulldozed the buildings, and then the entire area—buildings, fields, and trees—was bombed to rubble, to nothingness.

Schell didn't write extensively about the technicalities of the military operation. He wrote about the peasants who were removed from the village and the American soldiers who removed them. When describing the villagers, he wrote with a sort of delicate, restrained compassion, without pretending to understand their suffering or their thoughts any more than he did. And when he described the American soldiers and officers whom he met, he was not at all unsympathetic to them. And of course there are certain writers who clearly despise their fellow countrymen (Thomas Bernhardt comes to mind). But Schell was not one of them. He generally seemed to like the military men he encountered. It's just that what they were doing was appalling.

Plucked from the farms, small towns, and slums where they had lived in the United States, and where up until a few months earlier they had worked in factories or barns or shops or offices, packing shirts in boxes or selling greeting cards to familiar customers, the draftees and even the officers of the American military had awakened to find that they'd been dropped down into a land that for them was as strange and alien and uncanny as a dream—a land they knew nothing about, where they were surrounded by people whose words, gestures, and expressions they couldn't interpret. These American soldiers were not malevolent or vicious. At least as Schell met them in 1966, when the American part of the war was just beginning, they didn't really seem terribly different from the fresh-faced, smiling, gum-chewing, candy-distributing American GIs greeted as liberators by people in many countries at the end of World War Two. They certainly comprised an army much less deliberately cruel, much less motivated by hatred, than many we all know about. They were fairly nice young men. The problem was only that they had absolutely no idea why they were there in Vietnam; they had no idea of what they were supposed to do there; they had no idea what sort of danger these Vietnamese peasants could possibly pose to their own American families back home; they had no idea what their enemy was fighting for; and they had no idea why they were supposed to kill certain Vietnamese peasants but not others, and what exactly it was about those they were assigned to kill that made them worthy of death. To call the American soldiers racist would not be exactly inaccurate, but the more important fact was that they were situated inside an enormous multibillion-dollar operation that was entirely based on the unquestioned assumption that the Vietnamese peasants weren't very bright and could be easily manipulated. In other words, the somewhat well-meaning American soldiers arrived knowing nothing about the place to which they'd been sent, and the few things they then were told about it by their superiors were wrong. So they were very confused. Schell clearly portrays the early signs of the frustration and rage to which their confusion would lead in a couple of years, resulting ultimately in the shooting of American officers by their own men and the deliberate, crazed massacres of entire peasant villages by out-of-control American troops.

Roughly speaking, the first half of Schell's piece shows that indeed the American military, equipped with well worked out principles of military organization and brilliantly constructed machines for transporting people and for blowing things up, did a very good job of accomplishing its basic military objective, which was to remove the village of Ben Suc from the face of the earth so that it could not be used by the enemy as a base or refuge. It's in the second half of the book that we learn how bad a job the Americans did when called upon to answer the question inevitably posed by their successful destruction of the village, namely: What were they going to do with all the people who had lived there? And how were they going to do it in a way that would actually please the villagers, that would earn their loyalty and support, that would win over, in the phrase of the time, their "hearts and minds"—that would persuade the villagers, in other words, that the people who had just destroyed their village and killed their family members were in fact their friends? Because this was the ultimate objective of the American invasion of Vietnam. The American establishment in Washington and the soldiers on the ground both contrived in a way to be oblivious to the fact, to forget the fact, that people generally don't like to be ruled by foreigners, and that to persuade people who've been invaded and occupied by a foreign army to feel a loyalty to that army, to support that army, to risk their lives and die for that army—well, that couldn't be anything other than a very hard trick to pull off. All the same, a great many of those who were in charge of the American side of the war did have at least a vague understanding of the fact that without winning those hearts and minds they couldn't win the war. And in Schell's description of the miserably third-rate attempt of the American soldiers to construct a temporary camp for the villagers in the days after their village had been obliterated, we can see with perfect clarity why the Americans were indeed destined to lose the war, why Ho Chi Minh's forces would inevitably one day march into Saigon and rename it Ho Chi Minh City. In attempting to build this supposedly temporary camp for the villagers, the soldiers and officers of the American army behaved the way unmotivated people with lousy jobs do in any mediocre, low-morale office in any mediocre, low-morale business back home. They did the minimum required. But that wasn't enough to win over many hearts or minds.

The Vietnamese revolutionaries were fighting for their own country, for their own families. The Americans were not. They didn't know what they were fighting for. They did what they were told to do, and as Schell shows almost poignantly, they pretended to each other, and they pretended to themselves, that they were doing a pretty good job. The only ones who weren't fooled were the Vietnamese. They weren't fooled at all.

In other words, Schell's book might have been the crystal ball that could have led American policymakers to realize that quasi-imperial American interventions of this type could not succeed in the contemporary world, and if the policymakers had read Schell's book and studied it carefully, who knows, maybe a million or more Vietnamese lives could have been saved, along with the lives of fifty thousand American soldiers, along with countless lives in Afghanistan and Iraq. Anyway, the policymakers who read the book—and of course there would have been a few who did—apparently didn't take the time to think through its pretty obvious implications.

It's fascinating and significant to note that slightly less than five years before "The Village of Ben Suc" appeared in *The New Yorker*, the same magazine had published a two-part piece by a writer who eventually became a close friend and almost a mentor of Schell, namely Hannah Arendt. And her piece, entitled "Eichmann in Jerusalem," introduced a phrase that would have to be called one of the most explosive four-word phrases ever coined: "the banality of evil." This phrase referred to Arendt's belief that monstrous crimes could be perpetrated by people who did not appear in any obvious way to be monsters—that indeed the murder of six million innocent Jews was principally carried out by ordinary bureaucrats who were motivated much more by the conventional desire of all employed workers to do their assigned task to the satisfaction of their bosses than they were by a fanatical hatred towards Jews. Arendt's thoughts and her four-word phrase provoked bitterness and fury, because they seemed to deny the more popular view—perhaps one could even say it's been the more popular view in all times and places—that there are bad people—bad individuals and bad groups—and that if only these individuals or groups could be contained or killed, then evil would disappear and the good people would be safe. Instead, Arendt seemed to present the possibility that villains could not be easily detected, did not know themselves to be villainous, were not necessarily insane or fanatical, and might actually not be that different from everyone else, and indeed she opened the door to the possibility (not that Arendt said or believed this herself) that perhaps even reasonably nice people—even we ourselves—could be involved in evil. And this is precisely what Schell shows us in *The Village of Ben Suc*. Americans have always liked to think of themselves as well-meaning, friendly, basically decent people. That wasn't entirely false in 1966, and it's not even entirely false now. But reading this book today, over half a century after it was written, over half a century since the village of Ben Suc was obliterated, and over ten years since Schell's death, I feel Schell's steady and questioning eye still staring at all the friendly but possibly overconfident Americans and all the people they've killed all around the world during those intervening years.

—WALLACE SHAWN

# THE VILLAGE OF BEN SUC

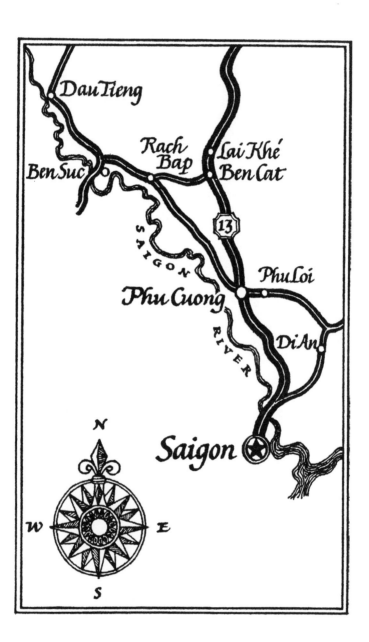

*I dedicate this book,*

*with love, to my parents*

UP TO A FEW months ago, Ben Suc was a prosperous village of some thirty-five hundred people. It had a recorded history going back to the late eighteenth century, when the Nguyen Dynasty, which ruled the southern part of Vietnam, fortified it and used it as a base in its campaign to subjugate the natives of the middle region of the country. In recent years, most of the inhabitants of Ben Suc, which lay inside a small loop of the slowly meandering Saigon River, in Binh Duong Province, about thirty miles from the city of Saigon, were engaged in tilling the exceptionally fertile paddies bordering the river and in tending the extensive orchards of mangoes, jackfruit, and an unusual strain of large grapefruit that is a famous product of the Saigon River region. The village also supported a small group of merchants, most of them of Chinese descent, who ran shops in the marketplace, including a pharmacy that sold a few modern medicines to supplement traditional folk cures of herbs and roots; a bicycle shop that also sold second-hand motor scooters; a hairdresser's; and a few small restaurants, which sold mainly noodles. These merchants were far wealthier than the other villagers; some of them even owned second-hand cars for their businesses. The village had no electricity and little machinery of any kind. Most families kept pigs, chickens, ducks, one or two cows for milk, and a team of water buffaloes for labor, and harvested enough rice and vegetables to sell some in the market every year. Since Ben Suc was a rich village, the market was held daily, and it attracted farmers from neighboring villages as well as the Ben Suc farmers. Among the people of Ben Suc, Buddhists were more numerous than Confucianists, but in practice the two religions tended to resemble each other more than they differed, both conforming more to locally developed village customs practiced by everyone than to the requirements of the two doctrines. The Confucianists prayed to Confucius as a Buddha-like god, the Buddhists regarded their ancestors as highly as any Confucianist did, and everyone celebrated roughly the same main holidays. In 1963, Christian missionary teams, including both Vietnamese and Americans, paid several visits to the village. One of these groups began its missionary work by slowly driving its car down the narrow main streets of the village, preaching through a loudspeaker mounted on the top of the car, and singing hymns accompanied by an accordion. Then, in the center of the village, a Vietnamese minister gave a sermon. He argued for the existence of God by pointing out that Vietnamese spontaneously cry out *"Troi oi!"* ("Oh God!") when they fall or get hurt, and told the villagers that their sins were as numerous as the particles of red dust that covered the leaves of the trees in the dry season. (The soil around Ben Suc is of a reddish hue.) Just as only God could wash every leaf clean by sending down a rainstorm, only God could wash away their countless sins. At the end of the sermon, he asked the villagers to kneel and pray, but none did. When he asked for questions, or even for arguments against what he had said, only the old village fool stepped forward to challenge him, to the amusement of the small group of villagers who had assembled to listen. Ordinarily, to entertain themselves, small groups of men would get together in the evening every two weeks or so to drink the local liquor—sometimes until dawn—and occasionally they would go fishing in the river and fry their catch together at night. Some of the marriages in the village were arranged and some were love matches. Although parents—particularly the girls' parents—didn't like it, couples often sneaked off in the evenings for secret rendezvous in the tall bamboo groves or in glades of banana trees. At times, there were stormy, jealous love affairs, and occasionally these resulted in fights between the young men. Parents complained that the younger generation was rebellious and lazy, and sometimes called their children *hu gao*—rice pots—who did nothing but eat.

Troops of the Army of the Republic of Vietnam (usually written "ARVN" and pronounced "Arvin" by the Americans) maintained an outpost in Ben Suc from 1955 until late 1964, when it was routed in an attack by the National Liberation Front (or N.L.F., or Vietcong, or V.C.), which kidnapped and later executed the government-appointed village chief and set up a full governing apparatus of its own. The Front demanded—and got—not just the passive support of the Ben Suc villagers but their active participation both in the governing of their own village and in the war effort. In the first months, the Front called several village-wide meetings. These began with impassioned speeches by leaders of the Front, who usually opened with a report of victories over the Americans and the "puppet troops" of the government, emphasizing in particular the downing of helicopters or planes and the disabling of tanks. Two months after the "liberation" of the village, the Front repelled an attack by ARVN troops, who abandoned three American M-113 armored personnel-carriers on a road leading into the village when they fled. The disabled hulks of these carriers served the speakers at the village meetings as tangible proof of their claimed superiority over the Americans, despite all the formidable and sophisticated weaponry of the intruders. Occasionally, a badly burned victim of an American napalm attack or an ex-prisoner of the government who had been tortured by ARVN troops was brought to Ben Suc to offer testimony and show his wounds to the villagers, giving the speakers an opportunity to condemn American and South Vietnamese-government atrocities. They painted a monstrous picture of the giant Americans, accusing them not only of bombing villages but also of practicing cannibalism and slitting the bellies of pregnant women. The speeches usually came to a close with a stirring call for support in the struggle and for what was sometimes called "the full coöperation and solidarity among the people to beat the American aggressors and the puppet troops." The speeches were often followed by singing and dancing, particularly on important National Liberation Front holidays, such as the founding day of the Front, December 20th, and Ho Chi Minh's birthday, May 19th. At one meeting, the dancers represented the defeat of a nearby "strategic hamlet." Usually, some of the women from Ben Suc itself danced, after being instructed by dancers from the Front. During the first year of Front government, a group of village teen-agers formed a small band, including a guitar, a trumpet, and various traditional Vietnamese instruments, and played for the meetings, but toward the end of 1965 they were replaced by a professional itinerant band. In all its meetings to boost morale and rally the villagers, the Front attempted to create an atmosphere combining impassioned seriousness with an optimistic, energetic, improvised gaiety that drew the

7

villagers into participation. At every opportunity, it attempted to make the villagers aware of their own collective power and of the critical necessity of their support in winning the war.

The Front organized the entire village into a variety of "associations" for the support of the war effort. The largest were the Youth Liberation Association, the Farmers' Liberation Association, and the Women's Liberation Association. Each of these three associations met twice a month, and in times of emergency they met more often. At the meetings, leaders again reported news of recent victories and also delivered instructions from higher authorities for the coming month. The Youth Liberation Association exacted dues of one piastre (about three-quarters of a cent) a month. The usual duties of its members were to carry supplies and rice for the troops, build blockades to make the roads impassable to jeeps and slow for armored personnel-carriers, and dig tunnels, usually as bomb shelters for the village but sometimes as hideouts or hospitals for the Front's troops. Every once in a while, the members were called to the scene of a battle to remove the dead and wounded. The Farmers' Liberation Association asked for dues of two piastres a month. The farmers also had to pay the Front a tax of up to ten per cent of their harvest. Taxes were assessed on a graduated scale, with the richest farmers paying the most and the poorest paying nothing, or even receiving a welfare allotment. In its propaganda, the Front emphasized the fact that rich peasants, who had the most to lose from the Front's policy of favoring the poor as a "priority class," would not be allowed to slip out of their obligations to the war effort or to play a merely passive role in it. Soldiers were recruited from both the Youth Association and the Farmers' Association, with members of the priority class most often entrusted with positions as officers and leaders. In one case, the Front supported a young orphan on welfare until he became established as a farmer, and then made him a soldier and promoted him to the rank of squad commander within a few months. Generally speaking, rich families and families with relatives in ARVN were mistrusted and kept under close watch. The duties of members of the Women's Liberation Association were not fixed. They supported the war effort through a number of miscellaneous jobs, among them making clothes. A few young women served as nurses, helping roving Front doctors at a large underground hospital in the jungle, only a few miles from the village. On the non-military side, the Women's Association took a strong stand on the need to break the bonds imposed on women by the "dark feudal society" and to raise women to an equal position with men. There was no Front organization for old people—formerly the most influential group in village life. As an ex-member of the Farmers' Association has put it, the Front's policy toward old people was to "recruit them if they were smart" and otherwise leave them alone with their old ways. The activities of the three large associations were coordinated by the Village Committee, a group of three men in close contact with higher officials of the Front. The three men on the Village Committee were the village chief, who dealt with military and political matters; the village secretary, who dealt with taxes and supplies; and the education officer, who was responsible for the schools and the propaganda meetings. The Front was particularly diligent in establishing schools where the children, along with reading and their multiplication tables, learned anti-American slogans. In short, to the villagers of Ben Suc the National Liberation Front was not a band of roving guerrillas but the full government of their village.

In the two years between the Front's victory at Ben Suc and the beginning of 1967, both the war on the ground and what the Americans call the "air war" escalated rapidly throughout the area of Binh Duong Province bordering on the Saigon River. This was the period of the extensive American buildup in Vietnam, and at the villages of Di An, Lai Khé, Ben Cat, and Dau Tieng—all in the vicinity of Ben Suc—American and ARVN bases were either established or greatly expanded. Following its initial failure to retake Ben Suc, ARVN ran several more campaigns in the area, but in these it either failed to make contact with the enemy or was beaten back. A push by the American 173rd Airborne Brigade in October, 1965, failed to engage the enemy significantly. In late 1965, the Front permitted a team of ARVN troops to come into Ben Suc and attempt their own version of the Front's village meetings. This kind of ARVN meeting, which the Americans call a Hamlet Festival, is, like so many of the techniques employed by the South Vietnamese government and the United States Army, a conscious imitation of the Front's programs. (In a full-scale Hamlet Festival, troops will surround a village and order everyone into the center. Then, while intelligence men set up a temporary headquarters to interrogate the males caught in the roundup, searching for draft dodgers as well as for the enemy, a special team of entertainers will put on a program of propaganda songs and popular love songs for the women and children. Sometimes a medical team will give shots, hand out pills, and offer medical advice. Lunch is usually served from a mess tent. In the most abbreviated version of the Hamlet Festival, only a medical team will go into a village.) The fact that the Front allowed an ARVN medical team to enter the village in 1965 was quite consistent with the Front's continuing policy of deriving whatever benefit it can from government programs and facilities. One American official has noted, "If they don't try to blow up a certain power station, it usually means they're drawing power off it for themselves."

Between 1965 and 1967, American bombing of every kind increased tremendously throughout the Saigon River area. There were strikes with napalm and phosphorus, and strikes by B-52s, whose bombs usually leave a mile-long path of evenly spaced craters. As the

American bases grew, the amount of large artillery also increased. There is apparently a policy in Vietnam of never letting any big gun remain silent for more than twenty-four hours, and the artillery on many bases fires a certain number of rounds every evening. Ordinarily, before bombing or shelling, an American pilot or artillery man must obtain permission from the province chief, or district chief, who, as a Vietnamese, is presumed to be more familiar with the surroundings than the Americans and able to restrain them from destroying populated areas. However, in the case of Binh Duong Province in January of 1967 the province chief, himself a colonel in ARVN, who was from outside the province, had taken his post only three months before, and had never controlled most of the areas being bombed, so he knew less about the area than most of the Americans. In South Vietnam, certain areas have been designated Free Strike Zones, which means that no permission is needed to fire into them. These are usually unpopulated jungle areas in which the Front is suspected of operating at night. Most of the routine nightly fire is lobbed into these zones, where it blows up jungle trees and—the Americans hope—the caves and bunkers of the Front. As there was at least one Free Zone within a few miles of Ben Suc, the thump of incoming artillery shells jarring the ground became a regular feature of life in the village.

In the daytime, pilots of fighter-bombers are shown their targets by troops on the ground or by small propeller planes called bird dogs, which spot promising targets from the air. The fliers adhere to a policy of bombing populated areas as little as possible, but sometimes beleaguered ground troops will call in planes or artillery fire to destroy a village that is being defended by the Front. In such cases, if there is time, an attempt is made to warn the villagers, either by airborne loudspeakers or by leaflets dropped on the village. The United States Army's Psychological Warfare Office has many hundreds of different leaflets, designed for subtly different situations. On one side of Leaflet No. APO-6227, for instance, a cartoon drawing represents the long trajectory of a large shell from a ship at sea to an inland village, where a human figure has been blown into the air and a grass-roofed house is bursting into pieces under the impact of the explosion. On the other side is a message in Vietnamese, reading, "Artillery from our ships will soon hit your village. You must look for cover immediately. From now on, chase the Vietcong away from your village, so the government won't have to shell your area again."

The center of Ben Suc was bombed one morning in mid-1965. The bombs destroyed several two-story brick-and-mortar houses and wounded or killed more than twenty people, including several children. Some months before the bombing, the Front, to protect the center of the village, had made a mocking use of a new policy of the South Vietnamese government. Around that time, the government had publicly offered a guarantee that Allied troops would refrain from attacking any building or vehicle showing the government flag of three red stripes on a yellow ground. The purpose, as an American officer explained it, was to encourage the people to "associate safety with the national flag," for "it means something when everybody's going around carrying the national flag." In Ben Suc, however, the Front, moved by a spirit of irreverent humor quite typical of it at times, raised the government flag over a rice-storage house—more as a prank than as a serious preventive measure against bombings. For several months, it fluttered at the top of the storehouse—a bold joke, known through the whole village, and a brazen taunt to the government. The joke had a bitter ending when the center of the village was bombed and the rice storehouse destroyed. After this bombing, the Front government in Ben Suc moved about a hundred people from the center of the village to the outskirts, where they lived with relatives. It also laid explosive booby traps in various spots outside the village. The job of warning villagers away from these spots was entrusted to teams of teen-age girls. In addition, the Front encouraged families to dig out rooms beneath their houses as bomb shelters. Later, there were many bombings, and many casualties, in the fields outside the village—particularly near the river, where the bombing was most frequent. From Ben Suc halfway to the provincial capital of Phu Cuong, about fifteen miles down the river, the riverside fields were polka-dotted with craters of every size. At least a third of the small fields had been hit at least once, and some of the craters had turned entire fields into ponds. The bombing and the artillery fire were at their most intense in the early morning, when the Americans considered anything that moved highly suspicious, so the farmers took to starting work in the fields around eight or nine o'clock instead of at seven, as their custom had been. Not only the destruction but the crashing of bombs and shells nearby and in the distance made life continuously nerveracking, with everyone tensely ready to run to a bomb shelter at a second's notice. The Psychological Warfare Office sought to make the most of the fear and tension by stepping up the volume of the leaflets dropped on the area. In a booklet describing the leaflets available for these purposes, Leaflet No. AVIB-246, whose "theme" is listed as "scare," has a cartoon drawing on one side showing a soldier of the Front dying, his hands futilely clutching the air in front of him and his face in the dirt, while jet planes fly overhead, dropping bombs. The message on the other side reads, "Each day, each week, each month, more and more of your comrades, base camps, and tunnels are found and destroyed. You are shelled more often, you are bombed more often. You are forced to move very often, you are forced to dig deeper, you are forced to carry more loads away. You are tired, you are sick. Your leaders tell you victory is near. They are wrong. Only DEATH is near. Do you hear the planes? Do you hear the bombs? These are the

sounds of DEATH: your DEATH. Rally now to survive."
Another leaflet shows a photograph of the mutilated
corpse of a young man. His stomach and intestines are
flowing out of him onto the ground. The message on the
other side reads, "If you continue to follow the Vietcong, and destroy villages and hamlets, sooner or later
you will be killed, like Colonel Tran Thuoc Quong.
Colonel Quong will never need his belt again. He is
DEAD." The word "dead" is written in large block letters
that drip with blood. Some leaflets depict American
weapons with the teeth and claws of beasts, killing or
torturing people in the manner of the fantastic devils in
medieval paintings of Hell. The drawing on one leaflet
shows a tank with evil, slitted eyes, fangs, and long
mechanical arms with metal talons that reach out toward the viewer. The tank crushes one man under its
treads, squeezes drops of blood from a screaming
second man in its talons, and engulfs a third man in a
column of flame that spurts from between its dragon-
like fangs.

People from many villages around Ben Suc who had
been left homeless after ground battles, bombing, and
shelling migrated to the comparative safety of other
villages, to live with relatives or just fend for themselves. When the small village of Mi Hung, across the
river from Ben Suc, was heavily bombed, at least a
hundred of its people moved into Ben Suc. During
1966, a scattering of refugees from other bombed villages had also found their way there. Then, in the

second week of the month of January, 1967—when the population of Ben Suc was further swollen by relatives and friends from neighboring villages who had come to help with the harvest, which was exceptionally abundant that season, despite the war—the Americans launched in Binh Duong Province what they called Operation Cedar Falls. It was the largest operation of the war up to that time.

For the Americans, the entire Saigon River area around Ben Suc, including particularly a notorious forty-square-mile stretch of jungle known as the Iron Triangle, had been a source of nagging setbacks. Small operations there were defeated; large operations conducted there turned up nothing. The big guns shelled and bombed around the clock but produced no tangible results. The enemy "body count" was very low, and the count of "pacified" villages stood at zero. In fact, a number of villages that had been converted into "strategic hamlets" in Operation Sunrise, launched three years earlier, had run their government protectors out of town and reverted to Front control. Late in 1966, the American high command designed the Cedar Falls operation as a drastic method of reducing the stubborn resistance throughout the Iron Triangle area. Named after the home town, in Iowa, of a 1st Division lieutenant who had been posthumously awarded the Medal of Honor, Operation Cedar Falls involved thirty thousand men, including logistical support, and it was planned and executed entirely by the Americans, without the advance knowledge of a single Vietnamese in the province. The decision that *no* Vietnamese was a good enough security risk was based on previous experiences, in which the enemy had learned about operations ahead of time and had laid traps for the attackers or simply disappeared. It also reflected the Army's growing tendency to mistrust all Vietnamese, regardless of their politics. On several American bases, entrance is forbidden to all Vietnamese, including ARVN soldiers, after a certain hour in the evening. During Cedar Falls, security was particularly tight.

A plan was made to attack Ben Suc, but Ben Suc was regarded as an objective quite separate from the operation's principal target—the Iron Triangle. The Iron Triangle is a patch of jungle bounded on the west, for about thirteen miles, by the Saigon River; on the east, also for about thirteen miles, by National Route No. 13; and on the north, for six miles, by a nameless smaller road. Ben Suc lay just beyond the northwest corner of the Triangle. Until the Cedar Falls operation, the Triangle long had a reputation as an enemy stronghold impenetrable to government troops, and had been said to shelter a full division of enemy troops and also a vast system of bunkers and tunnels used by the Front as headquarters for its Military Region IV, which surrounds the city of Saigon. American intelligence had also received reports of a twelve-mile tunnel running the length of the Triangle from north to south. The operation was the first move in a newly devised long-term war strategy in which large American forces would aim primarily at engaging the main forces of the enemy and destroying their jungle bases one by one, while ARVN troops would aim primarily at providing security for the villages thus freed from Front control. General Earle G. Wheeler, Chairman of the Joint Chiefs of Staff, who visited the area later, said, in an interview, "We must continue to seek out the enemy in South Vietnam—in particular, destroy his base areas where the enemy can rest, retrain, recuperate, resupply, and pull up his socks for his next military operation. . . . Primarily, the American units are engaged in search-and-destroy operations. In other words, they don't stay permanently in any given locale. . . . The Vietnamese military and paramilitary units are the ones which are used in the permanent security operations. The situation being what it is, General Westmoreland's first effort is to engage the Viet Cong main-force units and the North Vietnamese Army units and defeat them." He added, "The South Vietnamese forces are not ample enough to cope with the main-force units throughout the country. . . . I don't wish to imply that the South Vietnamese are not going to participate in the operations there. Of course they will. . . . This does not mean that all of the Vietnamese forces are going to be devoted to pacification. They can't be. And there's no intent for them to be. I just said a substantial portion."

According to the Cedar Falls plan, the Triangle was to be bombed and shelled heavily for several days both by B-52s and by fighter-bombers, and then blocked off around its entire thirty-two-mile perimeter with elements of the 1st Infantry Division along the northern edge, elements of the 196th Light Infantry Brigade along the river, on the west side, and elements of the 173rd Airborne Brigade along Route 13, on the east side. Together, these troops would man a hundred and sixty pieces of artillery. After the jungle had been heavily shelled and bombed, the 1st Division troops were to flatten the jungle in fifty-yard swaths on both sides of the road, using sixty bulldozers airlifted in by the huge, two-rotor Chinook helicopters. Then they were simultaneously to destroy the villages of Rach Bap, Bung Cong, and Rach Kien, evacuate the villagers, and start cutting broad avenues in the jungle with special sixty-ton bulldozers nicknamed hogjaws. These drives would be supported by air strikes and artillery barrages against the jungle. American troops would enter the Triangle behind the bulldozers, in an attempt to engage the enemy division that was rumored to be there and destroy the enemy headquarters.

The attack on Ben Suc was planned for January 8th—the day before the thrust into the Triangle. I joined a group of six newsmen outside a field tent on the newly constructed base at the village of Lai Khé, to hear Major Allen C. Dixon, of the 173rd Airborne Brigade, outline the plan and purpose of this part of the operation. "We have two targets, actually," he explained, pointing to a map propped on a pile of sandbags. "There's the Iron Triangle, and then there's the village of Ben Suc. This village is a political center, as far as the V.C. is concerned, and it's been solid V.C. since the French pulled out in '56. We haven't even been able to get a census taken in there to find out who's there." Most of the American officers who led the operation were not aware that ARVN had had an outpost in Ben Suc for the nine years preceding 1964. They saw the village as "solid V.C. as long as we can remember." Major Dixon continued, "Now, we can't tell you whether A, B, and C are at their desks or not, but we *know* that there's important infrastructure there—what we're really after here is the infrastructure of the V.C. We've run several operations in this area before with ARVN, but it's always been hit and run—you go in there, leave the same day, and the V.C. is back that night. Now, we realize that you can't go in and then just abandon the people to the V.C. This time we're really going to do a thorough job of it: we're going to clean out the place completely. The people are all going to be resettled in a temporary camp near Phu Cuong, the provincial capital down the river, and then we're going to move *everything* out—livestock, furniture, and all of their possessions. The purpose here is to deprive the V.C. of this area for good. The people are going to Phu Cuong by barge and by truck, and when they get there the provincial government takes over—it has its own

21

Revolutionary Development people to handle that, and U.S. AID is going to help."

A reporter asked what would happen to the evacuated village.

"Well, we don't have a certain decision or information on that at this date, but the village may be levelled," Major Dixon answered, and went on to say, "The attack is going to go tomorrow morning and it's going to be a complete surprise. Five hundred men of the 1st Infantry Division's 2nd Brigade are going to be lifted *right into* the village itself in sixty choppers, with Zero Hour at zero eight hundred hours. From some really excellent intelligence from that area, we have learned that the perimeter of the village is heavily mined, and that's why we'll be going into the village itself. Sixty choppers is as large a number as we've ever used in an attack of this nature. Simultaneous with the attack, choppers with speakers on them are going to start circling over the village, telling the villagers to assemble in the center of the town or they will be considered V.C.s. It's going to be hard to get the pilots on those choppers to go in low to make those announcements audible, but everything depends on that. Also, we're going to drop leaflets to the villagers." (Later, I picked up one of these leaflets. On one side, the flags of the Republic of Vietnam, the United States, the Republic of Korea, New Zealand, and Australia were represented in color; on the other side was a drawing of a smiling ARVN soldier with his arm around a smiling soldier of the National Liberation Front. The text, written in English, Vietnamese, and Korean, read, "Safe conduct pass to be honored by all Vietnamese Government Agencies and Allied Forces." I learned that the Chieu Hoi, or Open Arms, program would be in operation during the attack. In an attempt to encourage defections from the Front, the government was opening its arms to all *hoi chanh,* or returnees who turned themselves in. Hence the unusually friendly tone of the leaflets.)

About the encirclement of the village, Major Dixon said, "There are going to be three landing zones for the choppers. Then the men will take up positions to prevent people from escaping from the village. Five minutes after the landing, we're going to bring artillery fire and air strikes into the whole area in the woods to the north of the village to prevent people from escaping by that route. At zero eight thirty hours, we're going to lift in men from the 2nd Brigade below the woods to the south to block off that route. After the landing is completed, some of our gunships are going to patrol the area at treetop level to help keep the people inside there from getting out. After the area is secure, we're lifting a crew of ARVN soldiers into the center of the village to help us with the work there. We want to get the Vietnamese dealing with their own people as much as we can here. Now, we're hoping that opposition is going to be light, that we're going to be able to get this thing over in one lightning blow, but if they've got intelligence on this, the way they did on some of our other operations, they could have something ready for us and this *could* be a hot landing. It could be pretty hairy."

For several reasons, the plan itself was an object of keen professional satisfaction to the men who devised and executed it. In a sense, it reversed the search-and-destroy method. This time, they would destroy first and search later—at their leisure, in the interrogation rooms. After all the small skirmishes and ambushes, after months of lobbing tons of bombs and shells on vague targes in Free Strike Zones, the size, complexity, and careful coördination of the Cedar Falls operation satisfied the military men's taste for careful large-scale planning. Every troop movement was precisely timed, and there would be full use of air support and artillery, in a design that would unfold over a wide terrain and, no matter what the opposition might be, would almost certainly produce the tangible result of evacuating several thousand hostile civilians, thereby depriving the V.C. of hundreds of "structures," even if the "infrastructure" was not present. This time, unless the entire village sneaked off into the forest, the objective of the operation could not wholly elude the troops, as it had in previous campaigns. Thus, a measure of success was assured from the start. In concluding his briefing to the newsmen, Major Dixon remarked, "I think this really ought to be quite fascinating. There's this new element of surprise, of going right into the enemy village with our choppers and then bringing in our tremendous firepower. Anyway, it ought to be something to see."

That evening, I was sent by helicopter to a newly constructed base ten miles north of Ben Suc, at Dau Tieng, where Colonel James A. Grimsley, commanding officer of the 2nd Brigade, 1st Infantry Division, was winding up his briefing of his officers on the next morning's attack on Ben Suc. The officers were assembled in a tent, in which a single light bulb hung from the ceiling. "The purpose of this operation is to move in there absolutely as fast as we can get control of the situation," Colonel Grimsley said. "I want to emphasize that you're going to have only about ten seconds to empty each chopper, because another chopper will be coming right in after it. A last word to men landing below the southwest woods: Your job is to keep anyone from escaping down that way. Now, of course, if it's just a bunch of women and children wandering down through the woods, who obviously don't know what they're doing, don't fire, but otherwise you'll have to take them under fire. The choppers will be taking off at zero seven twenty-three hours tomorrow morning. Are there any questions?" There were no questions, and the officers filed out of the tent into the darkness.

The men of the 1st Division's 2nd Brigade spent the day before the battle quietly, engaging in few pep talks or discussions among themselves about the dangers ahead. Each man seemed to want to be alone with his thoughts. They spent the night before the attack in individual tents on the dusty ground of a French rubber plantation, now the Americans' new base at Dau Tieng. The airstrip was complete, but not many buildings were up yet, and construction materials lay in piles alongside freshly bulldozed roads. The men were brought in by helicopter in the afternoon from their own base and were led to their sleeping area among the rubber trees. Most of the transporting of American troops in Vietnam is done by helicopter or plane. So the men, hopping from American base to American base, view rural Vietnam only from the air until they see it through gunsights on a patrol or a search-and-destroy mission.

Darkness fell at about six-thirty. Thanks to a cloudy sky over the high canopy of rubber leaves, the area was soon in perfect blackness. A few men talked quietly in small groups for an hour or so. Others turned to their radios for company, listening to rock-'n'-roll and country-and-Western music broadcast by the American armed-services radio station in Saigon. The great majority simply went to sleep. Sleep that night, however, was difficult. Artillery fire from the big guns on the base began at around eleven o'clock and continued until about three o'clock, at a rate of four or five rounds every ten minutes. Later in the night, along with the sharp crack and whine of outgoing artillery the men heard the smothered thumping of bombing, including the rapid series of deep explosions that indicates a B-52 raid. Yet if the outgoing artillery fire had not been unusually near—so near that it sent little shocks of air against the walls of the tents—the sleepers would probably not have been disturbed very much. Because artillery fire is a routine occurrence at night on almost every American base in Vietnam, and because everyone knows that it is all American or Allied, it arouses no alarm, and no curiosity. Furthermore, because most of it is harassment and interdiction fire, lobbed into Free Strike Zones, it does not ordinarily indicate a clash with the enemy. It does make some men edgy when they first arrive, but soon it becomes no more than a half-noticed dull crashing in the distance. Only the distinctive sound of mortar fire—a popping that sounds like a champagne cork leaving a bottle—can make conversations suddenly halt in readiness for a dash into a ditch or bunker. Throughout that night of January 7th, the roaring of one of the diesel generators at the base served as a reminder to the men that they were sleeping on a little island of safety, encircled by coils of barbed wire and minefields, in a hostile countryside.

The men got up at five-thirty in the morning and were guided in the dark to a mess tent in a different part of the rubber grove, where they had a breakfast of grapefruit juice, hot cereal, scrambled eggs, bacon, toast, and coffee. At about six-thirty, the sky began to grow light, and they were led back to the airstrip. Strings of nine and ten helicopters with tapered bodies could be seen through the treetops, filing across the gray early-morning sky like little schools of minnows. In the distance, the slow beat of their engines sounded soft and almost peaceful, but when they rushed past overhead the noise was fearful and deafening. By seven o'clock, sixty helicopters were perched in formation on the airstrip, with seven men assembled in a silent group beside each one. When I arrived at the helicopter assigned to me—No. 47—three engineers and three infantrymen were already there, five of them standing or kneeling in the dust checking their weapons. One of them, a sergeant, was a small, wiry American Indian, who spoke in short, clipped syllables. The sixth man, a stocky infantryman with blond hair and a red face, who looked to be about twenty and was going into action for the first time, lay back against an earth embankment with his eyes closed, wearing an expression of boredom, as though he wanted to put these wasted minutes of waiting to some good use by catching up on his sleep. Two of the other six men in the team were also going into combat for the first time. The men did not speak to each other.

At seven-fifteen, our group of seven climbed up into its helicopter, a UH-1 (called Huey), and the pilot, a man with a German accent, told us that four of us should sit on the seat and three on the floor in front, to balance the craft. He also warned us that the flight might be rough, since we would be flying in the turbulent wake of the helicopter in front of us. At seven-twenty, the engines of the sixty helicopters started simultaneously, with a thunderous roar and a storm of dust. After idling his engine for three minutes on the airstrip, our pilot raised his right hand in the air, forming a circle with the forefinger and thumb, to show that he hoped everything would proceed perfectly from then on. The helicopter rose slowly from the airstrip right after the helicopter in front of it had risen. The pilot's gesture was the only indication that the seven men were on their way to something more than a nine-o'clock job. Rising, one after another, in two parallel lines of thirty, the fleet of sixty helicopters circled the base twice, gaining altitude and tightening their formation as they did so, until each machine was not more than twenty yards from the one immediately in front of it. Then the fleet, straightening out the two lines, headed south, toward Ben Suc.

In Helicopter No. 47, one of the men shouted a joke, which only one other man could hear, and they both laughed. The soldier who had earlier been trying to catch a nap on the runway wanted to get a picture of the sixty helicopters with a Minolta camera he had hanging from a strap around his neck. He was sitting on the floor, facing backward, so he asked one of the men on the seat to try to get a couple of shots. "There are sixty choppers here," he shouted, "and every one of them costs a quarter of a million bucks!" The Huey flies with its doors open, so the men who sat on the outside seats were perched right next to the drop. They held tightly to ceiling straps as the helicopter rolled and pitched through the sky like a ship plunging through a heavy sea. Wind from the rotors and from the forward motion blasted into the men's faces, making them squint. At five minutes to eight, the two lines of the fleet suddenly dived, bobbing and swaying from the cruising altitude of twenty-five hundred feet down to treetop level, at a point about seven miles from Ben Suc but heading away from it, to confuse enemy observers on the ground. Once at an altitude of fifty or sixty feet, the fleet made a wide U turn and headed directly for Ben Suc at a hundred miles an hour, the helicopters' tails raised slightly in forward flight. Below, the faces of scattered peasants were clearly visible as they looked up from their water buffalo at the sudden, earsplitting incursion of sixty helicopters charging low over their fields.

All at once, Helicopter No. 47 landed, and from both sides of it the men jumped out on the run into a freshly turned vegetable plot in the village of Ben Suc—the first Vietnamese village that several of them had ever set foot in. The helicopter took off immediately, and another settled in its place. Keeping low, the men I was with ran single file out into the center of the little plot, and then, spotting a low wall of bushes on the side of the plot they had just left, ran back there for cover and filed along the edges of the bushes toward several soldiers who had landed a little while before them. For a minute, there was silence. Suddenly a single helicopter came clattering overhead at about a hundred and fifty feet, squawking Vietnamese from two stubby speakers that stuck out, winglike, from the thinnest part of the fuselage, near the tail. The message, which the American soldiers could not understand, went, "Attention, people of Ben Suc! You are surrounded by Republic of South Vietnam and Allied Forces. Do not run away or you will be shot as V.C. Stay in your homes and wait for further instructions." The metallic voice, floating down over the fields, huts, and trees, was as calm as if it were announcing a flight departure at an air terminal. It was gone in ten seconds, and the soldiers again moved on in silence. Within two minutes, the young men from No. 47 reached a little dirt road marking the village perimeter, which they were to hold, but there were no people in sight except American soldiers. The young men lay down on the sides of embankments and in little hollows in the small area it had fallen to them to control. There was no sign of an enemy.

For the next hour and a half, the six men from No. 47 were to be the masters of a small stretch of vegetable fields which was divided down the center by about fifty yards of narrow dirt road—almost a path— and bounded on the front and two sides (as they faced the road and, beyond it, the center of the village) by several small houses behind copses of low palm trees and hedges and in back by a small graveyard giving onto a larger cultivated field. The vegetable fields, most of them not more than fifty feet square and of irregular shape, were separated by neatly constructed grass-covered ridges, each with a path running along its top. The houses were small and trim, most of them with one side open to the weather but protected from the rain by the deep eaves of a thatch-grass roof. The houses were usually set apart by hedges and low trees, so that one house was only half visible from another and difficult to see from the road; they were not unlike a wealthy American suburb in the logic of their layout. An orderly small yard, containing low-walled coops for chickens and a shed with stalls for cows, adjoined each house. Here and there, between the fields and in the copses, stood the whitewashed waist-high columns and brick walls of Vietnamese tombs, which look like small models of the ruins of once-splendid palaces. It was a tidy, delicately wrought small-scale landscape with short views—not overcrowded but with every square foot of land carefully attended to.

Four minutes after the landing, the heavy crackle of several automatic weapons firing issued from a point out of sight, perhaps five hundred yards away. The men, who had been sitting or kneeling, went down on their bellies, their eyes trained on the confusion of hedges, trees, and houses ahead. A report that Mike Company had made light contact came over their field radio. At about eight-ten, the shock of tremendous explosions shattered the air and rocked the ground. The men hit the dirt again. Artillery shells crashed somewhere in the woods, and rockets from helicopters thumped into the ground. When a jet came screaming low overhead, one of the men shouted, "They're bringing in air strikes!" Heavy percussions shook the ground under the men, who were now lying flat, and shock waves beat against their faces. Helicopter patrols began to wheel low over the treetops outside the perimeter defended by the infantry, spraying the landscape with long bursts of machine-gun fire. After about five minutes, the explosions became less frequent, and the men from the helicopters, realizing that this was the planned bombing and shelling of the northern woods, picked themselves up, and two of them, joined by three soldiers from another helicopter, set about exploring their area.

Three or four soldiers began to search the houses behind a nearby copse. Stepping through the doorway of one house with his rifle in firing position at his hip, a solidly build six-foot-two Negro private came upon a young woman standing with a baby in one arm and a little girl of three or four holding her other hand. The woman was barefoot and was dressed in a white shirt and rolled-up black trousers; a bandanna held her long hair in a coil at the back of her head. She and her children intently watched each of the soldier's movements. In English, he asked, "Where's your husband?" Without taking her eyes off the soldier, the woman said something in Vietnamese, in an explanatory tone. The soldier looked around the inside of the one-room house

33

and, pointing to his rifle, asked, "You have same-same?" The woman shrugged and said something else in Vietnamese. The soldier shook his head and poked his hand into a basket of laundry on a table between him and the woman. She immediately took all the laundry out of the basket and shrugged again, with a hint of impatience, as though to say, "It's just laundry!" The soldier nodded and looked around, appearing unsure of what to do next in this situation. Then, on a peg on one wall, he spotted a pair of men's pants and a shirt hanging up to dry. "Where's *he?*" he asked, pointing to the clothes. The woman spoke in Vietnamese. The soldier took the damp clothing down and, for some reason, carried it outside, where he laid it on the ground.

The house was clean, light, and airy, with doors on two sides and the top half of one whole side opening out onto a grassy yard. On the table, a half-eaten bowl of rice stood next to the laundry basket. A tiny hammock, not more than three feet long, hung in one corner. At one side of the house, a small, separate wooden roof stood over a fireplace with cooking utensils hanging around it. On the window ledge was a row of barley sprouting plants, in little clods of earth wrapped in palm leaves. Inside the room, a kilnlike structure, its walls and top made of mud, logs, and large stones, stood over the family's bedding. At the rear of the house, a square opening in the ground led to an underground bomb shelter large enough for several people to stand in. In the yard, a cow stood inside a third bomb shelter, made of tile walls about a foot thick.

After a minute, the private came back in with a bared machete at his side and a field radio on his back. "Where's your husband, huh?" he asked again. This time, the woman gave a long answer in a complaining tone, in which she pointed several times at the sky and several times at her children. The soldier looked at her blankly. "What do I do with her?" he called to some fellow-soldiers outside. There was no answer. Turning back to the young woman, who had not moved since his first entrance, he said, "O.K., lady, you stay here," and left the house.

Several other houses were searched, but no other Vietnamese were found, and for twenty minutes the men on that particular stretch of road encountered no one else, although they heard sporadic machine-gun fire down the road. The sky, which had been overcast, began to show streaks of blue, and a light wind stirred the trees. The bombing, the machine-gunning from helicopters, the shelling, and the rocket firing continued steadily. Suddenly a Vietnamese man on a bicycle appeared, pedalling rapidly along the road from the direction of the village. He was wearing the collarless, pajamalike black garment that is both the customary dress of the Vietnamese peasant and the uniform of the National Liberation Front, and although he was riding away from the center of the village—a move forbidden by the voices from the helicopters—he had, it appeared, already run a long gantlet of American soldiers without being stopped. But when he had ridden about twenty yards past the point where he first came in sight, there was a burst of machine-gun fire from a copse thirty yards in front of him, joined immediately by a burst from a vegetable field to one side, and he was hurled off his bicycle into a ditch a yard from the road. The bicycle crashed into a side embankment. The man with the Minolta camera, who had done the firing from the vegetable patch, stood up after about a minute and walked over to the ditch, followed by one of the engineers. The Vietnamese in the ditch appeared to be about twenty, and he lay on his side without moving, blood flowing from his face, which, with the eyes open, was half buried in the dirt at the bottom of the ditch. The engineer leaned down, felt the man's wrist, and said, "He's dead." The two men—both companions of mine on No. 47—stood still for a while, with folded arms, and stared down at the dead man's face, as though they were giving him a chance to say something. Then the engineer said, with a tone of finality, "That's a V.C. for you. He's a V.C., all right. That's what they wear. He was leaving town. He had to have some reason."

The two men walked back to a ridge in the vegetable field and sat down on it, looking off into the distance in a puzzled way and no longer bothering to keep low. The man who had fired spoke suddenly, as though coming out of deep thought. "I saw this guy coming down the road on a bicycle," he said. "And I thought, you know, Is this it? Do I shoot? Then some guy over there in the bushes opened up, so I cut loose."

The engineer raised his eyes in the manner of someone who has made a strange discovery and said, "I'm not worried. You know, that's the first time I've ever seen a dead guy, and I don't feel bad. I just don't, that's all." Then, with a hard edge of defiance in his voice, he added, "Actually, I'm glad. I'm glad we killed the little V.C."

Over near the copse, the man who had fired first, also a young soldier, had turned his back to the road. Clenching a cigar in his teeth, he stared with determination over his gun barrel across the wide field, where several water buffaloes were grazing but no human beings had yet been seen. Upon being asked what had happened, he said, "Yeah, he's dead. Ah shot him. He was a fuckin' V.C."

At about nine o'clock, people from outlying areas of the village began to appear on the road, walking toward the village center and bringing with them as many pieces of furniture, bicycles, pots, chickens, pigs, cows, ducks, and water buffalo as they could carry or herd along. At this point, the young mother also left her house, with her children, and started along the road. But about five minutes later she reappeared, with only the baby. She was walking in the forbidden direction, and several soldiers who saw her looked at each other questioningly as she passed. Arriving at her house, she encountered the tall soldier she had first met, and began a long explanation in Vietnamese, in a highly irritated tone. Then, rummaging in the laundry bag, she pulled out a woman's light-blue wallet and produced identification papers to show the soldier. She had returned for these. Still talking in an explanatory tone, in a loud voice, she returned to the line of villagers. Particularly at first, women and children predominated in the line. One woman carried a shoulder pole with her belongings balanced in a basket hanging on one end and a baby sitting in a basket on the other end. The villagers walked with slow, careful steps, looking straight in front of them. Some slowed their pace and turned their heads slightly when they passed the open-eyed corpse in the ditch, but none stopped and none showed any emotion. This procession, like the appearance of the houses, made it plain that Ben Suc was a wealthy village. Most of the villagers wore clean, unpatched clothing. The children had rosy cheeks and stout limbs. The cows were fat and sleek, and a great number of pigs and chickens were left rooting and pecking in deserted yards.

As the villagers passed, machine-gun fire rang out across the vegetable fields once more, this time accompanied by shouting. A few feet from where the cyclist had fallen, a soldier stood firing from the hip into a cluster of houses and trees. Twenty yards away, the sergeant of his unit, enraged, was yelling at him, "Git on back here! Git on back here! Do you hear? Killin' the fuckin' water buffalo! Fartin' around killin' the fuckin' water buffalo!" But the soldier did not look back or move. Again he fired, and a water buffalo in a small yard twenty feet away sank silently to its knees, then rolled over on its side. The sergeant swore and again shouted several times for the soldier to come back, but the soldier continued to peer toward the cluster of houses, holding his gun ready, in a challenging stance, as though there still might be something threatening there. After twenty seconds, he walked back to the furious sergeant. During this episode, the villagers did not break step but allowed themselves to turn their heads just enough to observe the proceedings. A few minutes later, a thin middle-aged man dressed in black, with long, straight hair that stuck out from his head at a number of angles, came down the road, looking freely from side to side and walking with a jauntier step than the other villagers. He was headed toward the center of the village. At one point, he stopped in the road to look directly at a group of Americans. The soldier with the cigar, who had first fired on the cyclist, told the man next to him, "That bastard better watch out. If he starts to run, he's going to get it in the head." At nine-thirty, new orders came, and the men abandoned their road to defend a wider perimeter around the village.

Following the villagers in toward the schoolhouse, I observed that all the houses had newly constructed bomb shelters both inside and outside—for animals as well as people. Noticing these, one American officer remarked that he wished ARVN would construct its bunkers as strongly. In back of a small temporary schoolhouse was a whole maze of trenches—presumably enough to hold the entire student body. In front of the school, a wooden signboard posted on a large tree bore the hand-lettered legend, in both Vietnamese and English, "If anyone aggresses your fatherland, enslaves you, what will you say to it?" Later in the morning, after hesitating a moment for fear the sign might be booby-trapped to explode if he touched it, a soldier took it down, asking a companion, "Hey, do you think this will make a good souvenir?"

At the center of the village was a small square, where three narrow roads intersected. Around it were eight or ten two-story brick houses, but most of them were in disrepair and had obviously been abandoned a long time ago. The first floor of one building, which had a sign on it in Vietnamese reading "Pharmacy," had no front, and the floor inside the single room was covered with debris. In several places, charred wrecks of buildings rose only slightly above their foundations. The roads in this area were blocked at regular intervals by low mounds of earth that would prevent a car but not a bicycle from passing. A sign posted on a tree exhorted in Vietnamese, "1. Battle vigorously against the American aggressors. 2. Develop the revolutionary force. 3. Develop solidarity among the people to win freedom and independence."

By ten o'clock, about a thousand villagers had assembled in an L formed by two fifty-foot-long roofless and half-ruined masonry buildings, near the center of the village, that had once been used as a school. The buildings faced a large pasture, which was now serving as a landing pad for a continuous stream of helicopters. The sky was clear and blue except for a few cottony clouds sailing low on the horizon in a strong, warm wind from the north. Bombs continued to crash in the jungle, sometimes no more than a half mile away, and they sent up large puffs of smoke—white for phosphorus, black for napalm. The soldiers watched with fascination as three jets, evenly spaced, made a wide circle and took turns at dive-bombing the forest to the southwest with napalm. Each came right over the village at the beginning of its dive, and the canisters of napalm were clearly visible as they sped earthward from the bellies of the dart-shaped planes.

Vietnamese soldiers, who had been lifted in by United States helicopters after the center of the village had been made secure, were directing still more villagers to the gathering point in front of the schoolhouse. Throughout Operation Cedar Falls, the pattern was to fly in ARVN troops after the initial fighting was over, so that they might search the villages, perform manual labor such as loading captured rice into bags, and carry on the administrative work of organizing the villagers. It was felt that the presence of ARVN troops would divert the villagers' feelings of awe at the operation from the American troops and toward its proper object, the government of South Vietnam. Perhaps the most important role of the ARVN troops, however, was to serve as a link between the Americans and the villagers. The task of crossing the language barrier between Vietnamese and English devolves squarely on ARVN troops. A number of American officers have undergone an intensive Army six-week language-training program, but—if only because of the exceptional difficulties of learning a language whose vocabulary has no common root with English and, furthermore, is pronounced "tonally," so that the same syllable can have many, often hilariously unrelated, meanings, according to its inflection and pitch—even the most linguistically talented students learn only basic constructions, adequate for dealing with only very simple situations. Every once in a while, with a display of uneasy shyness, an officer brings out a few words of Vietnamese, but if these ask a question, he more often than not listens to the answer in blank incomprehension. As the tour of duty in Vietnam is ordinarily no more than one year, very few Americans become fluent in Vietnamese. At Ben Suc, I found just one who was able to put his Vietnamese to practical use. For the most part, the Americans dealt with the Vietnamese soldiers, and the Vietnamese soldiers dealt with the people.

42

Except at the temporary headquarters, the American soldiers, the Vietnamese soldiers, and the villagers remained in almost entirely separate groups throughout the day of the attack. The villagers sat waiting, with nothing to do, among their kitchen utensils, hastily wrapped bundles, and animals. Beaks, legs, and wings of chickens protruded from the open mesh of large baskets into which they had been thrust. In accordance with village custom, children under about three years old wore nothing below the waist. Children from about seven up were used to working along with the adults. Now they carried heavy loads on shoulder poles, or held strings tied to the front legs of pigs. The women went barefoot, walked with a practical, flat-footed stride, and tied their bundles with the deft, unhesitating movements of people for whom physical labor is second nature. Standing in the schoolyard, each mother seemed wholly engrossed in keeping her children near her and looking after her animals and possessions, and carefully avoided turning her eyes toward her captors. The men were less concerned with the children, and their eyes moved behind sullen, cold masks, observing the Americans and the fate of their village, but they said nothing. To the untrained American eye, Vietnamese men, being slight and often beardless, appear younger than they are. A man in his late twenties may look like a teen-ager. This is particularly true in the villages, where the men usually wear their hair in a long, straight shock that looks boyish to Americans.

Whenever an American soldier or a Vietnamese soldier approached the throng of villagers, several of the older people smiled, folded their arms, and bowed, displaying what seemed an almost automatic deference toward these new authorities. The younger people never bowed or smiled. Some of the Americans had continued to guard the perimeter, but another group had set up tents in the pasture across the road from the old schoolhouse. Throughout the morning and the early afternoon, a special team of Americans detonated numerous booby traps and land mines that had been found around the village, with the result that there were no American casualties at Ben Suc. After digging trenches as a precaution against a mortar attack, the men mostly went to sleep in the sun or inside their tents. A few, who had been lifted in later in the morning, listened to popular songs on transistor radios or read their mail. Another part of the pasture was a busy helicopter landing pad. All day, enormous Chinook helicopters landed with supplies and took off again, blasting everyone with a gale of leaves, pebbles, and dust.

Having completed an initial search of the village, most of the Vietnamese soldiers had few immediate tasks to perform. Some simply lay on the ground and laughed, and others engaged in playfully aggressive games. Soldiers sparred with each other, and there was one loudly cheered wrestling match. At lunchtime, several of the ARVN soldiers gravitated to the center of the village, where they took a teapot and some food from one of the houses and cooked themselves a quick snack. One brought an old guitar out of a house and strummed the instrument clumsily, to the amusement of his friends. Two other soldiers got a fit of the giggles giving each other rides in a rickety wheelbarrow. One of the few unofficial contacts between American and Vietnamese soldiers took place when an American with a camera had the two pose with their wheelbarrow. One sat in the wheelbarrow and the other held the handles, and both momentarily put on fierce, stern expressions for the photograph.

In the middle of this relaxed, almost drowsy scene, the temporary command post was humming with activity. On the field radio, between bursts of static, calm, slow voices brought fresh orders and news of the rest of the operation. Though bombs continued to crash in the woods and smoke to rise on the horizon, they no longer created an impression of urgency but seemed wholly routine. The American soldiers showed only a technical interest in identifying the planes that passed overhead and guessing the kind of explosive used from the sound of the explosion and color of the smoke. The American arsenal is so varied that this game requires a subtle ear and considerable experience. "There goes a B-52 raid," a soldier would say. Or "That's outgoing artillery." Or "That's napalm."

With most of the populace assembled in one place, the Americans launched two projects that were a source of intense pride to the men in the field—a mess tent and a field hospital, both for the villagers. It is a cliché among the American military in Vietnam that "there are two wars in Vietnam": the military war, to provide security against the enemy, and what is usually called "the other war"—the war to "win the hearts and minds of the people." On the one hand, resolutely destroy the enemy; on the other hand, rebuild and reform. To the soldiers at Ben Suc, the hospital and the mess tent represented an essential counterweight to the killing and destruction. They saw the two installations as "the other half" of what they had done that morning. As one soldier put it, with astonishment, as if he were wondering whether this wasn't carrying benevolence to the enemy *too* far, "Our hospitals are full of V.C. at forty dollars a day. Just this morning, there was a woman who got shot up real bad. Both her legs were broken. A real mess. And they dusted her off in a chopper to the military hospital. We dusted off another little V.C. this morning." He shook his head and smiled at the idea of an army that tried to save the lives of an enemy it had just been trying to kill.

The hospital tent and the mess tent were set up side by side at one edge of the pasture. An officer explained to me that treatment was available not only to those wounded during the attack but to anyone, whatever his ailment. A team of Vietnamese doctors was to be lifted in later in the day to treat the patients—again in order to give the villagers the impression that this was a

Vietnamese project, not an American one. Meanwhile, in the hot morning sun, the tent walls of the hospital were open on all sides, and a young man who had been shot in one leg lay quietly on a cot, his eyes glassy and still. A young American medic in his shirtsleeves said that between ten and twenty villagers had been brought in for treatment—most of them children with minor skin diseases. He remarked on the exceptional good health of the Ben Suc villagers, but he went on to say that earlier that morning a distraught woman had brought a sick baby to a Vietnamese Army doctor, who had diagnosed the disease as malaria and had immediately administered an anti-malaria shot. The baby's condition had declined rapidly, and within two hours it had died. The American medic speculated that the baby had been allergic to the shot, and concluded that this incident helped to explain a subsequent reluctance among the villagers to come to the hospital tent. The mess tent was operated entirely by Americans. At noon, the villagers were offered a lunch of hot dogs, Spam, and crackers, served with a fruit-flavored beverage called Keen. Keen, a sweet drink made by dissolving a colored powder in water, is served on many American bases in Vietnam. Again, however, the turn-out was less than a hundred; perhaps there had been propaganda from the Front warning that the Americans would try to poison the villagers, or perhaps the villagers were seeking to keep all involvement with their captors to a minimum. In the late morning, one Ameri-

47

can infantryman offered sticks of gum to a few of the assembled children, and it was several minutes before the children overcame their fear sufficiently to dart forward for the gift.

With the attack over, the tricky task of distinguishing V.C.s from the civilians moved from the battlefield into the interrogation room. First, under the direction of the Americans, ARVN soldiers segregated the villagers by age level, sex, and degree of suspiciousness. All males between the ages of fifteen and forty-five were slated to be evacuated to the Provincial Police Head-quarters in the afternoon. From among them, all who were suspected of being Vietcong and a smaller group of "confirmed V.C.s" were singled out. Some of these men were bound and blindfolded, and sat cross-legged on the ground just a few yards from the large as-semblage of women, children, and aged. They were men who had been caught hiding in their bomb shel-ters or had otherwise come under suspicion. One group, for example, was unusually well dressed and well groomed. Instead of bare feet and pajamalike garb, these men wore Japanese foam-rubber slippers and short-sleeved cotton shirts. Standing over them, his arms akimbo, an American officer remarked, "No question about these fellas. Anyone in this village with clothes like that is a V.C. They're V.C.s, all right." A group of about a dozen men categorized as defectors were singled out to be taken to the special Open Arms center near Phu Cuong.

The Americans interrogated only the prisoners they themselves had taken, leaving the prisoners taken by the Vietnamese to the Vietnamese interrogators. The American interrogations were held in a large, debris-strewn room of the roofless schoolhouse. Four interrogating teams worked at the same time, each consisting of one American and an interpreter from the Vietnamese Army. The teams sat on low piles of bricks, and the suspects sat on the floor, or on one brick. These sessions did not uncover very much about the enemy or about the village of Ben Suc, but I felt that, as the only extensive spoken contact between Americans and the Ben Suc villagers throughout the Cedar Falls operation, they had a certain significance. Approximately forty people were questioned the first day.

In one session, a stout American named Martinez questioned, in a straightforward, businesslike manner, a small, barefoot, gray-haired man with a neat little gray mustache, who wore a spotlessly clean, pure-white loose-fitting, collarless shirt and baggy black trousers. First, Martinez asked to see the old man's identification card. By law, all South Vietnamese citizens are required to carry an identification card issued by the government and listing their name, date and place of birth, and occupation. (The Americans considered anyone who lacked this card suspicious, and a man who last registered in another village would have to supply a reason.) This suspect produced an I.D. card that showed him to be sixty years old and born in a village across the river. A search of his pockets also revealed an empty tobacco pouch and a small amount of money.

"Why did he come to Ben Suc?" Throughout the session, Martinez, who held a clipboard in one hand, spoke to the interpreter, who then spoke to the suspect, listened to his reply, and answered Martinez.

"He says he came to join relatives."

"Has he ever seen any V.C.?"

"Yes, sometimes he sees V.C."

"Where?"

"Out walking in the fields two weeks ago, he says."

"Where were they going?"

"He says he doesn't know, because he lives far from the center of the village. He doesn't know what they were doing."

"Does he pay any taxes?"

"Yes. The V.C. collect two piastres a month."

"What's his occupation?"

"He says he is a farmer."

"Let's see his hands."

Martinez had the man stand up and hold out his hands, palms up. By feeling the calluses on the palms, Martinez explained, he could tell whether the man had been working the fields recently. Aside from asking questions, Martinez employed only this one test, but he employed it on the majority of his suspects. He

50

squeezed the old man's palms, rubbed the calves of his legs, then pulled up his shirt and felt his stomach. The old man looked down uneasily at Martinez's big hands on his stomach. "He's not a farmer," Martinez announced, and then, with a touch of impatience and severity, he said, "Ask him what he does."

The interpreter talked with the suspect for about half a minute, then reported, "He says that recently he works repairing bicycles."

"Why did he say he was a farmer?"

"He says he has repaired bicycles only since he finished harvesting."

Deliberately accelerating the intensity of the interrogation, Martinez narrowed his eyes, looked straight at the suspect crouching below him, and, in a suddenly loud voice, snapped, "Is he a V.C.?"

"No, he says he's not," the interpreter announced, with an apologetic shrug.

Martinez relaxed and put his clipboard down on a table. A weary smile took the place of his aggressive posture. "O.K. He can go now," he told the interpreter.

The interpreter, a thin young man with sunglasses, who had spoken to the suspect in a courteous, cajoling manner throughout the questioning, seemed pleased that the interrogation was to involve nothing more unpleasant than this. He gave the old man a smile that said, "You see how nice the Americans are!" and then patted him on the shoulder and delivered him into the hands of a guard.

After the old man had gone, Martinez turned to me with the smile of a man who has some inside information and said confidentially, "He was a V.C. He was probably a tax collector for the V.C." After a moment, he added, "I mean, that's my supposition, anyway."

The other interrogations were very similar. Martinez asked the same questions, with little variation: "Where does he live?" "Is he a farmer?" (Then came the touch test.) "Has he seen any V.C.?" And, finally, "Is *he* a V.C.?" And the suspects, instead of insisting that the National Liberation Front actually governed the village and involved the entire population in its programs, supported him in his apparent impression that the Front was only a roving band of guerrillas. To judge by their testimony to Martinez, the villagers of Ben Suc knew the Front as a ghostly troop of soldiers that appeared once a fortnight in the evening on the edge of the forest and then disappeared for another fortnight. When one young suspect was asked if he had "ever seen any V.C.s in the area," he answered that he had seen "fifty armed men disappearing into the forest two weeks ago." Another man, asked if he knew "any V.C.s in the village," answered in a whisper that he knew of *one*—a dark-complexioned man about forty-five years old named Thang. Still another man said that he had been "taken into the jungle to build a tunnel a year ago" but couldn't remember where it was. I had the impression that the suspects were all veterans of the interrogation room. For one thing, they were able to switch immediately from the vocabulary of the Front to the vocabulary of the American and South Vietnamese-government troops. It is a measure of the deep penetration of propaganda into every medium of expression in wartime Vietnam that few proper names serve merely as names. Most have an added propagandistic import. Thus, to the Americans the actual *name* of the National Liberation Front is "Vietcong" (literally, "Vietnamese Communists")—a term that the Front rejects on the ground that it represents many factions besides the Communists. Likewise, to the Front the actual *name* of the Army of the Republic of Vietnam is "Puppet Troops." Even the names of the provinces are different in the two vocabularies. The Front refuses to comply with a presidential decree of 1956 renaming the provinces, and insists on using the old names—calling Binh Duong, for instance, by its old name of Thu Dau Mot. There is no middle ground in the semantic war. You choose sides by the words you use. The suspects made the necessary transitions effortlessly. (Confronted with this problem myself, I have tried in this article to use for each organization the name that its own side has chosen for it.)

Several women were brought into the schoolhouse for interrogation, sometimes carrying a naked child balanced astride one hip. Unlike the men, they occasionally showed extreme annoyance. One young woman only complained loudly, and did not answer any of the questions put to her. Her baby fixed the

53

interrogator with an unwavering, openmouthed stare, and an old woman, squatting next to the suspect, looked at the ground in front of her and nodded in agreement as the young mother complained.

"Do you know any V.C.s in this village?" the interrogator, a young man, asked.

The interpreter, having tried to interrupt the woman's complaining, answered, "She says she can't remember anything. She doesn't know anything, because the bombs were falling everywhere."

"Tell her to just answer the question."

"She says she couldn't bring her belongings and her pig and cow here." The interpreter shook his head and added, "She is very angry."

The interrogator's face grew tense for a moment, and he looked away, uncertain of what to do next. Finally, he dismissed the woman and impatiently turned his pad to a fresh sheet.

The Vietnamese troops had their own style of interrogation. At eleven o'clock that morning, an ARVN officer stood a young prisoner, bound and blindfolded, up against a wall. He asked the prisoner several questions, and, when the prisoner failed to answer, beat him repeatedly. An American observer who saw the beating reported that the officer "really worked him over." After the beating, the prisoner was forced to remain standing against the wall for several hours. Most of the ARVN interrogations took place in a one-room hut behind the school where the Americans were carrying on their interrogations. The suspects, bound and blindfolded, were led one by one into the hut. A group of ten or twelve fatherless families sitting under the shade of a tree nearby heard the sound of bodies being struck, but there were no cries from the prisoners.

As one young man was being led by one arm toward the dark doorway of the interrogation hut, a small boy who was watching intently burst into loud crying. I went inside after the suspect, and found that three tall, slender, boyish Vietnamese lieutenants, wearing crisp, clean American-style uniforms crisscrossed with ammunition belts, and carrying heavy new black pistols at their hips, had sat the young man against the wall, removed his blindfold, and spread a map on the floor in front of him. Pointing to the map, they asked about Vietcong troop movements in the area. When he replied that he didn't have the answers they wanted, one lieutenant beat him in the face with a rolled-up sheet of vinyl that had covered the map, then jabbed him hard in the ribs. The prisoner sat wooden and silent. A very fat American with a red face and an expression of perfect boredom sat in a tiny chair at a tiny table near the door, looking dully at his hands. The three lieutenants laughed and joked among themselves, clearly enjoying what seemed to them an amusing contest of will and wits between them and the silent, unmoving figure on the floor in front of them. Looking at the prisoner with a challenging smile, the lieutenant with the map cover struck him again, then asked him more questions.

55

The prisoner again said he couldn't answer. Suddenly noticing my presence, all three lieutenants turned to me with the wide, self-deprecating grins that are perhaps the Vietnamese soldiers' most common response to the appearance of an American in any situation. Realizing that I could not speak Vietnamese, they called in an American Intelligence officer—Captain Ted L. Shipman, who was their adviser, and who could speak Vietnamese fluently. They asked him who I was, and, upon learning that I was not a soldier but a reporter, they looked at each other knowingly, saluted me, and continued their interrogation, this time without beatings. A few minutes later, however, Captain Shipman, who had been standing beside me, said that he was extremely sorry but they wanted me to leave. When we were outside, Captain Shipman, a short man with small, worried eyes behind pale-rimmed glasses, drew me aside and, shaking his head, spoke with considerable agitation. "You see, they *do* have some—well, methods and practices that *we* are not accustomed to, that we wouldn't use if we were doing it, but the thing you've got to understand is that this is an Asian country, and their first impulse is force," he said. "Only the fear of force gets results. It's the Asian mind. It's completely different from what we know as the Western mind, and it's hard for us to understand. Look—they're a thousand years behind us in this place, and we're trying to educate them up to our level. We can't just do everything for them ourselves. Now, take the Koreans—

they've got the Asian mind, and they really get excellent results here. Of course, we believe that that's not the best way to operate, so we try to introduce some changes, but it's very slow. You see, we know that the kind of information you get with these techniques isn't always accurate. Recently, we've been trying to get them to use some lie detectors we've just got. But we're only advisers. We can tell them how we think they should do it, but they can just tell us to shove off if they want to. I'm only an adviser, and I've made suggestions until I'm *blue in the face!* Actually, though, we've seen some improvement over the last year. This is a lot better than what we used to have."

I asked if the day's interrogations had so far turned up any important information.

"Not much today," he answered. "They're not telling us much. Sometimes they'll just tell you, 'Hey, I'm a V.C., I'm a V.C.' You know—proud. Today, we had one old man who told us his son was in the V.C. *He* was proud of it." Then, shaking his head again, he said with emphasis, as though he were finally putting his finger on the real cause of the difficulty, "You know, they're not *friendly* to us at this place, that's the problem. If you build up some kind of trust, then, once some of them come over to your side, they'll tell you anything. Their brother will be standing near them and they'll tell you, 'Him? He's my brother. He's a V.C.' It's hard for us to understand their mentality. They'll tell you the names of their whole family, and their best friends thrown in." Of the Front soldiers he said, "They don't know what they're doing half the time. Outside of the hard-core leaders, it's just like those juvenile delinquents back home, or those draft-card burners. They're just kids, and they want excitement. You give those kids a gun and they get excited. Half of the V.C.s are just deluded kids. They don't know what they're doing or why. But the V.C. operates through terror. Take this village. Maybe everybody doesn't want to be a V.C., but they get forced into it with terror. The V.C. organizes an association for everyone—the Farmers' Association, the Fishers' Association, the Old *Grand-mothers'* Association. They've got one for everybody. It's so mixed up with the population you can't tell who's a V.C. Our job is to separate the V.C. from the people."

At that moment, a helicopter came in sight five hundred yards away, cruising low over the woods and emitting a steady chattering sound that was too loud to be the engine alone. Breaking off his explanation to look up, Captain Shipman said, "Now, there's a new technique they've developed. That sound you hear is the 7.62-calibre automatic weapon on the side. They have a hell of a time finding the V.C. from the air, so now when they hear that there's a V.C. in the area they'll come in and spray a whole field with fire. Then, you see, any V.C.s hiding below will get up and run, and you can go after them."

Captain Shipman went off to attend to other business, and I walked back to the interrogation hut. The fat American in the tiny chair was still looking at his hands, and the prisoner was still sitting stiff-spined on the floor, his lips tightly compressed and his gaze fixed in front of him. The young lieutenant with the map cover held it above the suspect's face and stared intently down at him. All three lieutenants were wholly engrossed in their work, excited by their power over the prisoner and challenged by the task of drawing information out of him. After twenty seconds or so, the American looked up and said to me, "They been usin' a little water torture." In the water torture, a sopping rag is held over the prisoner's nose and mouth to suffocate him, or his head is pushed back and water is poured directly down his nostrils to choke him. Again the lieutenants had not noticed me when I entered, and when the American spoke one of them looked up with a start. The tension and excitement in his expression were immediately replaced by a mischievous, slightly sheepish grin. Then all three lieutenants smiled at me with their self-deprecating grins, inviting me to smile along with them.

Captain Shipman came in, looking even more harried than before. One of the lieutenants spoke to him in a sugary, pleading tone, and Captain Shipman turned to me with a fatalistic shrug and said, "Look, I'm really sorry, but I get it in the neck if I don't take you away." Glancing over my shoulder as I left, I saw that the lieutenants were already crouching around their prisoner again and were all watching my exit closely.

Outside again, Captain Shipman explained that this was only a preliminary interrogation—that a more extensive session, by the Province Police, would be held later. He pointed out that American advisers, like him, would be present at the police interrogation.

At the end of an interrogation, the questioner, whether American or Vietnamese, tied an eight-inch cardboard tag around the neck of the bound prisoner. At the top were the words "Captive Card," in both Vietnamese and English, and below were listed the prisoner's name, address, age, occupation, and the kind of weapon, if any, he was carrying when caught. None of the captive cards on the first day listed any weapons.

At one o'clock, the official count of "V.C.s killed" stood at twenty-four, with no friendly casualties reported. Soldiers on the spot told me of six shootings. I learned that three men had crawled out of a tunnel when they were told that the tunnel was about to be blown up. "One of them made a break for it, and they got him on the run," the soldier said. An officer told me that a man and a woman were machine-gunned from a helicopter while they were "having a picnic." I asked him what he meant by a picnic, and he answered, "You know, a *picnic*. They had a cloth on the ground, and food—rice and stuff—set out on it. When they saw the chopper, they ran for it. They were both V.C.s. She was a nurse—she was carrying medical supplies with her, and had on a kind of V.C. uniform—and he was, you know, sitting right there with her, and he ran for it, too, when the chopper came overhead." A soldier told me that down near the river three men with packs had been shot from a distance. Inspection of their packs revealed a large quantity of medical supplies, including a surgical kit, anti-malaria pills, a wide assortment of drugs, and a medical diary, with entries in a small, firm hand, that showed the men to have been doctors. (The *Stars and Stripes* of January 12th gave an account of seven additional shootings: "UPI reported that Brigadier General John R. Hollingsworth's helicopter accounted for seven of the Vietcong dead as the operation began. The door gunner, personally directed by the colorful assistant commander of the 1st. Inf. Div., shot three V.C. on a raft crossing the Saigon River, another as he tried to sneak across camouflaged by lily-pads, and three more hiding in a creek nearby.")

I asked the officer tabulating the day's achievements how the Army disposed of enemy corpses. He said, "We leave the bodies where they are and let the people themselves take care of them." It occurred to me that this was going to be difficult, with only women and children left in the area. Later in the afternoon, I heard the following exchange on the field radio:

"Tell me, how should we dispose of the bodies, sir? Over."

"Why don't you throw them in the river? Over."

"We can't do that, sir. We have to drink out of that river, sir."

The captured-weapons count stood at forty-nine—

forty booby traps, six rifle grenades, two Russian-made rifles, and one American submachine gun. All were captured in caches in tunnels.

In the early afternoon, I went over to the field where the Americans were resting to ask them about the attack in the morning and what their feelings were concerning it. When I told one soldier that I was interested in finding out what weapons, if any, the Vietnamese dead had been carrying, he stiffened with pride, stared me straight in the eye, and announced, "What do you mean, 'Were they carrying weapons?' Of course they were carrying weapons! Look. I want to tell you one thing. *Anyone killed by this outfit was carrying a weapon.* In this outfit, no one shoots unless the guy is carrying a weapon. You've got to honor the civilian, that's all." With that, he terminated our conversation. Later, he and I walked over to a small tent where several men sat on the ground eating Spam and turkey from canned rations. They ate in silence, and, in fact, most of the men preferred to be alone rather than talk over the morning's attack. The men who did say anything about it laconically restricted themselves to short statements—such as "C Company had some light contact in the woods over there. Snipers mainly"—usually brought out in an almost weary tone, as though it were overdramatic or boastful to appear ruffled by the day's events. Nor did they kid around and enjoy themselves, like the ARVN soldiers. One young soldier, who looked to be not out of his teens, did come riding by on a small bicycle he had found near one of the houses in the village and cried out, with a big, goofy smile, "Hey! Look at this!," but the other men ignored him coldly, almost contemptuously.

I entered into conversation with Major Charles A. Malloy. "We're not a bunch of movie heroes out here," he said. "I think you'll find very few guys here who really hate the V.C. There's none of that stuff. I'll tell you what every soldier was thinking about when he stepped out of the helicopter this morning: Survival. Am I going to make it through? Am I going to see my wife and kids again? O.K., so some people without weapons get killed. What're you going to do when you spot a guy with black pajamas? Wait for him to get out his automatic weapon and start shooting? I'll tell you I'm not. Anyway, sometimes they throw away their weapon. They'll throw it into the bushes. You go and look at the body, and fifty yards away there's the weapon in the bushes. You can't always tell if they were carrying a weapon. Now, this man here has just heard that his wife had his first kid, a baby girl." He indicated a short, young-looking soldier with bright-red hair. "Now, if I told any one of these men they could go home tomorrow, they'd be off like a shot." The men listened with quiet faces, looking at the ground. "No, there's very little fanatic stuff here," he went on. At that moment, a middle-aged Vietnamese wearing the customary black floppy clothing was led by, his arms bound behind his back. Major Malloy looked over his shoulder at the prisoner and remarked, "There's a V.C. Look at those black clothes. They're no good for working in the fields. Black absorbs heat. This is a hot country. It doesn't make any sense. And look at his feet." The prisoner had bare feet, like many of the villagers. "They're all muddy from being down in those holes." In a burst of candor, he added, "What're you going to do? We've got people in the kitchen at the base wearing those black pajamas."

At three-forty-five, the male captives between the ages of fifteen and forty-five were marched to the edge of the helicopter pad, where they squatted in two rows, with a guard at each end. They hid their faces in their arms as a Chinook double-rotor helicopter set down, blasting them with dust. The back end of the helicopter was lowered to form a gangplank, leading to a dark, square opening. Their captive cards flapping around their necks, the prisoners ran, crouching low under the whirling blades, into the dim interior. Immediately, the gangplank drew up and the fat bent-banana shape of the Chinook rose slowly from the field. The women and children braved the gale to watch its rise, but appeared to lose interest in its flight long before it disappeared over the trees. It was as though their fathers, brothers, and sons had ceased to exist when they ran into the roaring helicopter.

Inside the Chinook, the prisoners were sitting on two long benches in a dim tubular compartment, unable to hear anything over the barely tolerable roaring of the engines, which, paradoxically, created a sensation of silence, for people moved and occasionally talked but made no sound. Many of the prisoners held their ears. Up front, on each side, a gunner wearing large earphones under a helmet scanned the countryside. The gunners' weapons pointed out, and there was no guard inside the helicopter. A few of the prisoners—some bold and some just young—stood up and looked out of small portholes in back of their seats. For the first time in their lives, they saw their land spread below them like a map, as the American pilots always see it: the tiny houses in the villages, the green fields along the river pockmarked with blue water-filled bomb craters (some blackened by napalm), and the dark-green jungles splotched with long lines of yellow craters from B-52 raids, the trees around each crater splayed out in a star, like the orb of cracks around a bullet hole in glass.

That night, the women, children, and old people were allowed to return to their houses under a guard of ARVN soldiers. Being of peasant stock themselves for the most part, the ARVN soldiers knew just how to catch, behead, and pluck a chicken. Most of the battalion helped itself to fried chicken—a rare luxury for them. In the hot sun the next day, they went inside the houses to keep cool. Except for the guards on the perimeter of the village, the Americans stayed apart in the field next to the landing pad; even so, a few of them managed to get some chicken to fry.

The next morning, trucks arrived in Ben Suc to begin the evacuation. The Americans on the scene were not sure just how many possessions the villagers were supposed to take with them. The original orders were to "bring everything." In practice, the villagers were allowed to take anything that they themselves could carry to the trucks. Families near the spot where a truck was drawn up took furniture, bedclothes, bags of rice, pigs, cooking utensils, agricultural tools, and just about anything else they wanted to, but, without their men to help them, families living at any distance from a truck could carry only clothing, a few cooking utensils, and one or two bags of rice. By government decree, any rice beyond fifteen bushels per family was to be confiscated as "surplus," potentially intended for the enemy, but although many families had as much as four times this amount at their houses, they could never carry more than fifteen bags with them to the trucks, so no scenes of confiscation took place at the loading. (During the next few days, all the cattle still in or near the village were rounded up and brought to join the villagers.) Several of the ARVN soldiers helped the women and children load the heavy pigs and bags of rice on the trucks. Later, an American officer who saw this exclaimed in amazement, "You saw it! The Arvins loaded those trucks. We've never seen anything like it."

ARVN's willingness to load and unload trucks during this whole operation became quite famous, evoking a few compliments for the ARVN troops amid the usual barrage of American criticism. Hearing about the truck-loading, another officer remarked, "You pat the little Arvin on the ass and he just might do a good job." Because the Americans were very eager to find the Front's storage places for the rice collected as taxes, they had a Vietnamese officer announce to the assembled women that by divulging where this rice was they would gain permission to take it with them to the resettlement area, but no one responded. Several Americans speculated about whether this showed loyalty to the Vietcong.

Jammed with people, animals, and bundles of possessions, the trucks left Ben Suc in convoys of ten. The first few miles of the journey took them along a bumpy dirt road in a choking cloud of dust, which quickly coated everything. After an hour, they turned onto another road, near Phu Cuong, and headed for Phu Loi, their destination. Finally, the trucks swung right into a vast field of at least ten acres, empty except for a row of a dozen or more huts standing in the shade of a line of low palm trees along a narrow dirt road. Since there was nothing resembling a camp for the villagers, the American drivers brought their charges to these huts—the only shelter in sight. They were the houses of families who farmed fields nearby and who were totally surprised to discover themselves playing host to several thousand strangers—strangers not only from Ben Suc but from several other villages. Earlier that day, truckloads of people from other villages in the Iron Triangle had been arriving in a steady stream. ARVN soldiers again won praise by helping to unload the trucks, and American soldiers also gave a hand with the unloading. Dusty, squealing, desperately kicking pigs were slid to the ground down ramps improvised from boards. One American soldier put his hands under the arms of a tiny, very old deaf woman and whisked her to the ground, setting her gently down as though she were as light as a bunch of straw. Several children smiled at seeing the old lady lifted down. As for the lady herself, she simply stood motionless among the pigs and rice bags, staring in front of her with blank unconcern; apparently she was too old to realize that she had just flown through the air from truck to ground. The Americans also lifted down several small, amazed, pantless children. After the unloading was finished, some of the Ben Suc people jammed themselves into the already jammed houses of the Phu Loi peasants, and others simply tried to find some shade. Soon they began to talk with the people from the other villages, who had their own tales of misfortune to tell.

Late in the morning of that day, I made my way to the northern edge of the Iron Triangle to see what was happening in these other villages. Arriving at a point near the northeastern tip of the Triangle at noon, I was offered a ride in a jeep with two Psychological Warfare officers and an Army photographer who were heading west across the top of the Triangle on a tour of inspection. Driving in the wake of heavy military traffic, we soon found ourselves in the midst of an immense demolition job being performed on a large rubber plantation, four villages, and large areas of the jungle itself. On both sides of the road, bulldozers had already pushed back the jungle for fifty yards, forming six miles of rough, hilly field that contained torn-up tree trunks, broken branches, and upturned stumps with their roots sticking out in every direction. In places, the stretch of road was alive with bulldozers, flashing yellow and silver in the forest and bobbing up and down in a hilly sea of mangled trees. Soldiers with machetes were walking down rows of tall, slender rubber trees and felling them at waist height, while engineers placed explosives around the brick buildings of the plantation managers. In the villages of Rach Kien, Bung Cong, and Rach Bap, the sequence of attack, evacuation, and demolition had been compressed into a single day. Across from the rubber plantation, the villagers crouched along the road with their bundles of belongings while American infantrymen ducked in and out of the palm groves behind them, some pouring gasoline on the grass roofs of the houses and others going from house to house setting them afire. When we came upon this, a major in my jeep exclaimed, "Oh, God, this is bad! This is like the Marines." Then, to the Army photographer, who had got out to take pictures, he called out, "Be careful not to get any of our men in those shots!" At the village of Rach Bap, many of the houses were already burned to the ground and bulldozers were crushing whatever was left standing. To find the houses, the bulldozers would plow into the groves of palm trees, snapping the trunks as they went, and then, discovering a house, crush it. Columns of heavy black smoke rose from the burning village. The villagers had been assembled next to a masonry building in the center of this activity, and the air around them was filled with the snapping of palm trunks and the high-pitched roar of the bulldozers cutting into the walls of a few masonry houses near the road. Standing or crouching without speaking, their faces drawn tight in dead masks, the people seemed not to see or hear what was happening around them.

At Rach Bap, I asked a captain in charge of one phase of the evacuation why it was necessary to destroy the villages and the jungle. "We're going to deprive the V.C. of lodging and food in this area!" he shouted over the noise of the bulldozers and of the explosions in the jungle. "We want to prevent them from moving freely in this area. By making these paths in the jungle, we're going to be able to see them a lot more easily than before. From now on, anything that moves around here is going to be automatically considered V.C. and bombed or fired on. The whole Triangle is going to become a Free Zone. These villages here are all considered hostile villages."

I asked what would happen to the men of Rach Bap.

"We're considering all the males in this district V.C., and the people as hostile civilians," he replied.

The term "hostile civilians" was a new one, invented during Operation Cedar Falls for the people in the villages that had been marked for destruction. The question of what to call these villagers was one of many semantic problems that the Army had to solve. At the scene of an evacuation, they usually used the phrase "hostile civilians," which hinted that all the villagers at least supported the enemy and thus all deserved to be "relocated." But later, at Phu Loi, the officials in charge reverted to the more familiar term "refugees," which suggested that the villagers were not themselves the enemy but were "the people," fleeing the enemy.

When I asked the captain at Rach Bap how the Army sorted out the enemy from the friendly civilians, he answered, "In a V.C. area like this one, there are three categories of classification. First, there are the straight V.C. They're the activists, the real hard core. Then, there are the V.C. sympathizers, who support the V.C. with taxes. Then, there's the . . . there's a third category. There are three categories. I can't think of the third just now, but I can say that there's no middle road in this war. Either you're with us or you're against us. We've captured eleven straight V.C.s and sixty-three suspects, and had thirty-two *hoi chanh*. The body count isn't in yet."

As we were driving in the vicinity of Rach Bap, our jeep pulled up next to a Vietnamese officer at the side of the road who was carrying an electric bullhorn on one shoulder and a submachine gun on the other. Hearing that I was a reporter, he introduced himself proudly in broken English. "I am Captain Nguyen Hué. I am district chief of Ben Cat area. I control forty-four thousand people. Now we chase away the V.C.—they never come back. If they come back today, O.K., but if don't come back—all killed!" District Chief Nguyen Hué had not been able to exercise real control over these villages until that day, and he could not look forward to controlling them in the future, because they would soon cease to exist. From what I saw later, I gathered that he was bent on squeezing a maximum of exercise of control out of his day and a half of authority. He drove around in a station wagon and frequently jumped out to give a short, excited lecture to groups of villagers crouching along the road waiting for the evacuation trucks. "I am Captain Nguyen Hué, district chief of the Ben Cat District," he told them, adding that he and the Americans had come to save them from the Vietcong and urging them to persuade their friends who were still hiding to give themselves up, because those who didn't would be killed.

Farther along, in an area that, according to the original plan, should already have been fully evacuated, one of two majors in our jeep noticed the figures of two little girls by the edge of the forest. Going into four-wheel drive, we lurched over the plowed stretch to where they were standing. Just beyond the border of the fifty-yard demolition, a number of tiny huts still stood in a grove of tall trees sloping down to rice fields along the river. The little girls appeared to be sisters, about nine and twelve years old. They were barefoot, wore simple, short beltless dresses, and had their black hair in long braids. A few yards away from them, a very old man and woman watched us approach. When we arrived, no one seemed quite sure how to deal with the situation. Then the two little girls took charge. Speaking slowly and clearly, and repeating everything several times, they informed a major who had attended six weeks of language school that their parents had been taken away in a truck and that they now wished to load their rice and furniture into a truck and go themselves. They laughed freely when the major failed at first to understand them. Without waiting for a response, they beckoned to us to follow them. One of the officers muttered, "Better watch it—it could be a trap," but the others followed the little girls. Upon reaching one of the huts, the girls hoisted onto their shoulders sacks of rice that I thought would surely crush them, and pointed to things for us to carry. One almost full bag of rice was open at the top. The younger sister gave me a handful of straw, indicating that I was to tie it closed. She watched me fumble for a

73

minute, and then took the straw from my hands and expertly twisted it around the top of the bag in a way that made it secure. They insisted on bringing a large jar full of rice that could be carried only when it was suspended by its wire handles from a pole and there was a person at each end to man the pole. I took one end and the sisters took the other, and we had just started toward the jeep when the pole snapped and the jar fell—without overturning—on the ground. The little girls burst out laughing, and it was a full fifteen seconds before the elder sister ran back for another pole. Meanwhile, an empty truck had been hailed and brought over to the edge of the forest. A minute later, I noticed that the little girls had disappeared. After a brief search, they were discovered out in the rice fields stuffing unwinnowed rice into burlap bags. They came immediately when the Vietnamese-speaking major called to them. One of the officers said that he had found a rowboat and wanted to blow it up with a hand grenade. While he was performing this mission, the other Americans loaded the rice on the truck and hoisted up the girls and the aged couple, who had fetched a few bundles themselves by this time. Holding their sleeves over their mouths against the dust, they set out down the road for Phu Loi. The officer who had gone to attend to the rowboat returned after an explosion had sounded from the woods, and reported that, to his surprise, the hand grenade had blown only a six-inch hole in the bottom of the skiff.

We pushed on in our jeep to the end of the plowed boulevard in the jungle, and here we came on five armored personnel-carriers sitting parked, facing the jungle in fan formation. Perched in the turrets of their massive vehicles, the men ate canned rations and kept an impassive eye on the edge of the jungle fifty yards away. On the high metal deck of one of the personnel-carriers, two monkeys no bigger than cats were tied with five-foot pieces of cord to the base of a machine gun. A soldier sitting in a turret above them alternately threw scraps of food to them and grabbed at them, so that they rushed screeching to the far ends of their cords. Sometimes, when the monkeys bared their teeth and chattered, the soldier would lean down, bare his own teeth, and cry "Nyahhh," terrifying the monkeys. Watching this from a distance, a young soldier who had just spent most of the morning in the area of the burning villages suddenly shouted, "I can't stand it! I just can't stand it! Whenever I see people with monkeys, they're always teasing them, or something. Always poking at them or annoying them. Why do they have to torture the monkeys? Why can't they just leave the monkeys alone?"

We returned across the top of the Triangle to Ben Cat, a village that was to be spared destruction. The people living in the vicinity of Ben Cat had already been "relocated" several times in the last five years, in an unsuccessful attempt to break the influence of the National Liberation Front in the area. Now, as trucks full of villagers poured out of the Triangle, the Army was using one of the smaller former resettlement areas as a headquarters and relay point for the villagers. The huts there were the architectural equivalent of a crazy quilt. Straw, bits of cardboard, corrugated iron, planks, flattened beer cans, mats of woven branches, burlap, and anything else thin and flat that might keep out rain were tied, nailed, pegged, and wired to crude frames made of tree trunks lashed together at the joints with vines or wire. A coil of barbed wire had been thrown around a half acre of these huts, and inside this enclosure the new homeless moved in with the old homeless and both groups mingled freely with the soldiers of the two armies. A heavy traffic of trucks, jeeps, tanks, carts, bulldozers, and armored personnel-carriers moved slowly through the enclosure, heading into the Iron Triangle. The children had quickly invented games involving the parked or slow-moving tanks and personnel-carriers. They climbed up on them and hung on the back for rides, to the annoyance of the American soldiers, who could not see all sides of their vehicles from their high turrets and were afraid that a child would slip under the treads. Several women and children from the village of Ben Cat had already set themselves up in business, selling bottled orange drinks and beer at more than sixty piastres a bottle (about fifty cents) to the parched and affluent Americans. Beyond this, however, there was little intercourse between the different groups in the enclosure. Carts drawn by water buffalo moved in the tracks left by tanks, and soldiers carrying submachine guns milled about among villagers lugging possessions, but each of them was on his own urgent errand, and they rarely communicated, or even looked at each other. Only the children, always curious, stared in wonder at all the new things. For a minority of the villagers, Ben Cat would be the permanent resettlement area. The majority were to be taken on to Phu Loi. Captain Nguyen Hué was to decide which families went and which stayed.

At Phu Loi, truckloads of villagers from the north end of the Triangle and from Ben Suc continued to arrive in front of the little row of huts in the huge field. On the first day, over a thousand people were brought in. When they climbed slowly down from the backs of the trucks, they had lost their appearance of healthy villagers and taken on the passive, dull-eyed, waiting expression of the uprooted. It was impossible to tell whether deadness and discouragement had actually replaced a spark of sullen pride in their expression and bearing or whether it was just that any crowd of people removed from the dignifying context of their homes and places of labor, learning, and worship, and dropped, tired and coated with dust, in a bare field would appear broken-spirited to an outsider.

The reason for the total lack of shelter and facilities for the villagers at Phu Loi when they arrived was simply that the Vietnamese who were to provide these knew nothing about their assignment until twenty hours before the influx began. On the morning of the attack on Ben Suc, Lieutenant Colonel Ly Tong Ba, the chief of Binh Duong Province, learned, to his surprise, that American troops had already set in motion a plan to destroy four villages in his province and evacuate the villagers to Phu Loi, where he was expected to provide them with what the Americans called a "refugee camp," and also with food, and with a form of security around the camp that would keep the villagers in as well as enemy organizers out. One AID official observed to me that day, "Refugees are a real headache. Nobody likes to have to take care of refugees." Colonel Ba was annoyed at being suddenly saddled with the tedious and thankless task of caring for anywhere from six thousand to ten thousand homeless, hostile villagers, but at the same time he was a little flattered when the Americans told him that they were thrusting on him a position of "command" in the largest operation of the Vietnam war. As the highest official of the South Vietnamese government in the province, he was to assume responsibility for villagers recently freed from Communist domination. The Americans had taken care of the "military half," and now it was up to him to lead "the other war—for the hearts and minds of the people," which could be really won only by "the Vietnamese themselves." His first task, they said, was to come out to the battlefield in a helicopter and talk to the people. They explained that they had been unable to inform him of the operation earlier because the security risk forbade their telling any local Vietnamese about it, and that they had been unable to do anything more than stockpile rice at an AID warehouse in preparation for the camp because any major construction would have given the operation away to the enemy. However, because Province Chief Ba was acquainted so late with the nature of his task, several officials from AID who knew the details of the operation thoroughly and had already decided on the site for the construction of the camp were assigned to him to suggest plans of action. These officials were very clear on the point that all credit for building the camp was to go to the Vietnamese—that, from that point on, "Vietnamese had to deal with Vietnamese." Explaining the policy later, Philip L. Carolin, Jr., and chief AID official for Phu Cuong, said, "We can't do it for them. They have to learn to do it themselves someday. One of our most important jobs here is to teach these people to stand on their own feet. Otherwise, what's going to happen when we leave?" Colonel Ba, therefore, soon overcame his initial pique and became an enthusiastic promoter of the operation as well as its commander. At times, perhaps thrilled by his sudden direct connection with the Americans' awesome military power and by his own vital role in its operations, he exaggerated the aims of the current project, indulging in bursts of enthusiasm as he talked to reporters. On the second day, after the villagers began to arrive, he triumphantly announced to

79

four assembled American correspondents, "We are going to destroy everything in the Iron Triangle. Make it into a flat field. The V.C. can no longer hide there." Actually, instead of flattening the entire area of forty square miles, the Americans restricted themselves to bulldozing several wide avenues across the jungle.

Although two AID officials were brought in from other provinces expressly to help with the construction of the camp, the principal full-time AID official was Carolin, a big man of twenty-eight, with curly blond hair and a young, almost collegiate sunburned face with a small turned-up nose. He had worked in Vietnam for six months after teaching history and doing social work in the United States. Temporarily superseding him in the hierarchy of American officials, however, was a man introduced to me as "Lieutenant Colonel Kenneth J. White, province representative for the Office of Civilian Operations, and top civilian in the area." When I asked him how it came about that the top civilian was a colonel, he explained that he was "on loan from the Army" for the period of the camp's establishment. Because the United States Army 1st Division would supply most of the building supplies and the ARVN 5th Division would do most of the construction, the Americans felt that a man of high military rank would get faster results as top civilian than a full-time civilian would. I asked him how he liked being a civilian. "This is my first stretch as a civilian," he answered. "You find that certain things just don't get done the way you're used to." A cheerful man of trim, athletic build, Colonel White is thirty-seven, and in talking business he speaks so rapidly that you wonder if he's going to be able to get all the words out. He maintained a buoyant enthusiasm throughout the construction of the camp. Whether he was offering advice to Colonel Ba, in a self-consciously humble, soft-spoken manner, or moving from task to task with his characteristic rapid, almost bounding gait, he displayed unflagging energy and almost unclouded high spirits, not unlike an eager camp councillor managing a large and difficult but highly successful jamboree.

Since there was no central advance plan for the camp, it grew through hundreds of separate improvised decisions taken by a great number of organizations, with the Vietnamese organizations reporting to Colonel Ba and the American organizations reporting to Colonel White. On the Vietnamese side, there were the province administration, the ARVN 5th Division, the Revolutionary Development teams, and, arriving later in the week, several Vietnamese groups formed for "nation building." On the American side, there were the Army's 1st Division, AID, the sizable American advisory group to the ARVN 5th Division, and the American advisers to other Vietnamese organizations, like the Province Police. There was also a team of Philippine doctors. In speaking of the planning of the camp, Colonel White remarked, "We're winging it all the way!"

As a site for the camp, AID had chosen the empty

field at Phu Loi. Fronting on the road, it was bordered on one side and at the back by forest, and on the other side by barracks for the ARVN 5th Division's thousands of dependents. This housing consisted of long, straight rows of unpainted wooden sheds divided into compartments, each with a doorway but rarely a door. In between the rows, the earth was bare except for an occasional vegetable patch. Like so much of wartime Vietnam, particularly in and around the cities, the dependents' area had a rough, half-finished look, as though it were just being built, or were being torn down. It had been made by simply flattening the previous landscape and laying out the structures according to a strictly symmetrical crosshatch plan. There had been no attempts at beautification by either the builders or the inhabitants. The ARVN dependents were displeased at having to live in the neighborhood of the dirty, impoverished new arrivals, and they tried without much success to keep their children from going over to watch the soldiers at work. Later, when they spotted a movie screen inside the camp during the showing of a propaganda film, a few of the women indignantly demanded to know why the enemy people were shown movies and the loyal supporters had none.

At the moment that the Ben Suc villagers got off the trucks at Phu Loi, the military plan that had started with the attack on Ben Suc and had proceeded precisely on schedule came to an end. This was the point in the plan at which the villagers came under the control of the provincial authorities. But Colonel Ba and his advisers were not yet ready to assume control, and the result was a planless interlude of about a day. Colonel Ba and Colonel White managed to borrow men from the United States 1st Division and the ARVN 5th while they waited for the Revolutionary Development workers to arrive, but these men were unprepared for their brief assignment, and the tight guard that had been mounted over the "hostile civilians" until that day all but faded away. Any of the villagers who wished to escape could easily have done so at this point, and any outsider could easily have come to join them. At about three o'clock, the 1st Division parked a water truck with spigots in the yard of one of the absurdly jammed houses under the row of palms. Mothers and children crowded around it with pots and pitchers, and soon six inches of mud had formed under their feet. Several mothers thrust bawling babies directly under a spigot to wash them, or made their children stand under the streams of water. A medical tent was set up as at Ben Suc, and next to it blossomed a yellow nylon pavilion, shaped like a circus tent, with chairs and a table in its shade. This was referred to as the "command tent," but most of the commanders were too busy arranging for the construction of the camp to sit down. At one point in the late afternoon, three weary locally recruited Revolutionary Development workers, wearing cowboy hats, availed themselves of the chairs and the shade to take a rest. Shortly after they had sat down, an old woman in

83

black, with bare feet and straggling hair, came shuffling toward them, talking angrily to herself. Upon reaching the threesome, she focussed her annoyance on them. She said that she wanted to go back to Rach Bap to get a baby that she had left there. The three R.D. men looked uncomfortable, and one answered with resigned politeness that they could do nothing just then, and that she should ask some soldiers standing by a truck. The old woman walked away muttering, and did not speak to the soldiers.

In the evening, as Colonel Ba began to mobilize his forces, coils of barbed wire were unrolled around the villagers wherever they had squatted down, and guards were posted, signalling the end of the planless interlude. The attempt to provide security was still only halfhearted, though. (I accompanied an American major on a tour of the grounds that evening, and in the darkness we passed through two barbed-wire barriers without being challenged. The guards we did encounter did not seem to know whether they were keeping the villagers in or the enemy out. The major thought they should face outward, and reprimanded one, a Vietnamese, for failing to do so.) As the sun set, the warmth left the dry air, and the light dimmed quickly in the unclouded sky. A few small cooking fires sprouted up among the villagers as some of them prepared a supper of the rice they had brought with them, and a low sound of talking rose from the dark field.

A hundred yards away, soldiers of the ARVN 5th

Division set up floodlights and began construction of the camp. That afternoon, bulldozers had flattened several hundred cone-shaped anthills, six feet high, which had covered the site for the camp, leaving an expanse of several acres of level earth. On this the Vietnamese soldiers first erected a long, peak-roofed frame of bamboo poles, fastened together with pieces of wire. The frame was of the most basic simplicity, having no supports or poles that would not appear in a child's line drawing of a three-dimensional transparent rectangular house. Over this the soldiers pitched a single hundred-foot piece of nylon cloth and pegged it down on each side with ropes and stakes, thus forming a roof over the frame and completing the structure. The final product was a long nylon canopy over the bare earth, without floors or walls. Around ten o'clock, having constructed five or six of these canopies, the ARVN soldiers roused several hundred villagers from their resting places in the dark and led them through a gap in a long barbed-wire fence circling the canopies and into the harshly lighted construction area. Each family was assigned a space about ten feet square between the vertical poles that held up the nylon. At eleven o'clock, the soldiers turned out the lights. That night, the temperature dropped into the low fifties, making sleep difficult for the villagers, most of whom lay, without blankets, on mats or in the dust itself. About five hundred people remained in the field outside the camp.

With no walls to keep out the light, the people under the canopies were awakened at six-thirty by the sun, to find themselves in one corner of a vast earthen expanse enclosed by barbed wire and guarded by a few tired soldiers standing, singly, around them in the early-morning light. They noticed that the canopy over them was gaily colored red and white, the two colors alternating every twenty feet. Now helpless to do anything for themselves, they began a life of sitting and waiting. Not long after they awoke, a little gray truck on which were mounted two speakers facing in opposite directions began to pass up and down inside the barbed wire, blaring loud, cheerful Vietnamese music into the camp. After several runs back and forth, the driver stopped the truck and slumped exhausted in the front seat, fighting off drowsiness as the day grew hot and the music played on. The music consisted of a number of songs performed in the rapid, high, inflected nasal style of Vietnamese popular singers. The lyrics praised the government in Saigon and urged the people to pitch in and help with the reconstruction of their country. The songs, interspersed with propaganda tapes on which a warm, vigorous, manly voice boomed questions and a chorus of young voices shouted answers in unison, were played again and again.

Under the canopies, the people had embarked on a common existence with their animals. Because the vertical poles supporting the canopies were the only places where the big, gray, muddy, bristle-backed pigs could be tied, it was impossible to keep them from entering the compartments to escape the burning sun. The animals were everywhere and in everything. If the people grew tired and quiet as they got hungry, the animals became more and more aggressive and active. A ravenous, snorting pig would occasionally break its tether and range wide in search of food, sometimes finding it in a villager's unprotected store. And the chickens, now released from their baskets, ran everywhere, pecking at anything that looked like food. The pure, high peeping of baby chicks rose on all sides as flocks of the little creatures raced at breakneck speed down the fresh bulldozer tracks, their fuzz blending into the yellow earth so that they were difficult to see. Later in the day, as the heat grew more intense, the animals calmed down a bit—especially the pigs, which keeled over on their sides and lay panting in the dust.

By official calculation, there were almost three times as many women as men in the camp, and almost twice as many children as adults. On the morning after the construction began, the camp held about a thousand people, approximately seven hundred of them children. Growing restless with nothing to do, the children old enough to walk but too young to know where they were going tended to drift away from their compartments, sometimes following a chicken or a dog, sometimes with no purpose at all. Soon, wandering among the identical canopies, they would stop, look about them, and start crying for their mothers. (On the first day, the mothers could often find their lost children themselves, but in succeeding days, as the population rose to nearly six thousand, this became impossible. When Vietnamese Revolutionary Development teams arrived on the scene, two days later, returning these lost children constituted one of their major jobs.)

The ARVN soldiers resumed the construction of canopies at about nine-thirty in the morning. They also constructed a temporary latrine, consisting of two fifteen-yard parallel ditches, one for men and one for women, divided from each other and also surrounded by a waist-high fence of gleaming silver corrugated iron. The entire arrangement, including the interior, was visible from the busy main entrance to the camp, which was not more than fifty yards away. The designers of this mass toilet apparently intended its users to balance themselves on the brink of the ditch in order to relieve themselves into it. This latrine got very little use. Instead, most of the villagers restrained themselves until dark and then slipped out beyond the lighted part of the camp to a place where the bulldozed earth had been left in rough hills and mounds. But there was no grass or brush cover within the bounds of the barbed wire, and on the first day under the canopies a few of the old people, who could not stand to relieve themselves semi-publicly, sneaked through the barbed wire in search of brushy, protected areas outside the coils. This became considerably more difficult on the second day, when two coils of barbed wire were added to the first to form a barbed-wire pyramid—two coils on the bottom and one on top. The children slipped in and out with no trouble, but the old people required help. The helper would part the wires while the escaper entered the inner coil and attempted to negotiate the inner wall between the two coils himself, with the helper unhitching him from the wire if he got stuck. One afternoon, I came upon an old woman caught on the barbs on the inside of the inner coil and a boy about eight years old attempting to free her by reaching into the coil. When I approached, the little boy jumped back and the old woman's eyes filled with panic, but she produced a thin smile, and then, stuck inside the coil, attempted to bow to me. Speaking to my interpreter, she explained that she had been relieving herself in the brush outside the camp. The ARVN guards, although they could not condone these temporary escapes outright, apparently adopted a lenient policy toward them.

Arriving at the camp early in the morning of the first day dressed in a freshly ironed plaid sports shirt and a cowboy hat, against the sun, Colonel White met informally with two AID officials and, looking out at the newly constructed red-and-white canopies fluttering in a fresh breeze under a flawless blue sky, exclaimed, "This is wonderful! I've never seen anything like it. It's the best civilian project I've ever seen." Throughout, the camp was referred to as a "civilian project" or as "the civilian half of what we're doing here." "We've got shelter up for almost a thousand people here in one

89

day," the Colonel went on. "The ARVN boys have been working just like coolies loading and unloading those trucks. It's been highly gratifying." Then, suddenly remembering something, he waved an arm between the tall shoulders of the AID officials in the direction of an officer of the South Vietnamese Army who was standing half outside the ring of Americans and focussing his whole attention on an attempt to grasp Colonel White's rapid English. The shoulders parted, and the officer, whose beret hardly reached the chins of the Americans, was startled out of his single-minded concentration. "This is Lieutenant An," Colonel White announced, extending his hand to one side and smiling warmly down at the Lieutenant as though he were introducing someone to a television audience. All eyes moved to Lieutenant An, and Colonel White continued dramatically, "Here's the man who did it. Here's the man who deserves the credit." Lieutenant An nodded, his eyes following Colonel White's lips in a desperate but futile attempt to understand. "He did a wonderful job with his men. He deserves all the credit." Noticing the Lieutenant's confusion, Colonel White ran through the words of praise again, trying to warm up a smile that he had been wearing too long already. "He did a wonderful job. His men stayed up until eleven o'clock doing this last night. We didn't do anything. He deserves the credit." Recognizing that attention was centered on him, Lieutenant An stepped forward with a smile. There was a silence. Colonel White turned to the

Americans again and said, "About the water trucks
. . ." Lieutenant An stepped back, and the shoulders
closed. After the two AID officials had left, Colonel
White paused, again looked out over the coils of barbed
wire toward the bright canopies, and, turning to Philip
Carolin, said with warm satisfaction, "You know, Phil,
sometimes it just feels *right.*"

Colonel Ba, when he arrived, was no less exuberant
than Colonel White. He stationed himself in the round
yellow command tent, which had been moved to a
point near the main entrance to the camp. His men
brought several more chairs, another table, a large map
of the Iron Triangle, and a small cooler containing beer
and soft drinks on ice. Colonel Ba, a short, powerful
man who gestured strongly with his arms and usually
faced the world through a pair of sunglasses, was
clearly in a state of eager excitement. He issued a
stream of orders and talked with gusto to American
reporters in broken English, frequently laughing
abruptly at his own remarks, although there did not
always seem to be any joke. His American advisers
politely murmured suggestions to him, almost as
though their presence were a secret. American reporters repeatedly turned to Colonel White to ask questions, but usually the Colonel tactfully redirected them
to Colonel Ba. As soon as a public-address system had
been set up to supplement the sound truck, Colonel Ba
had a microphone installed in his command tent. This
put him in direct contact with the villagers, none of

whom had heard the voice of any official representing the government in Saigon for two years. In addition to official announcements, Colonel Ba took care of many small problems and interrupted the taped propaganda to make extemporaneous announcements of his own. He took particular pleasure in announcing the names and descriptions of lost children in an attempt to find their parents. On the second day of the camp's existence, a Vietnamese soldier moved down the aisles between the canopies, blasting insecticide on the villagers and their belongings from a machine that resembled a large rotary lawnmower. There was a mild panic among the villagers, who had been told by the Front that American defoliant sprays were poisonous to people. To reassure them, Colonel Ba went to his microphone and announced, "Don't worry! The poison will not harm you. It kills only insects. The Vietcong say the government and the Americans will poison you, but instead we improve your welfare by killing the insects." Then, turning to two reporters seated in his tent, he said, "You see? The Vietcong say we will kill the people, but instead the poison kills only the insects!" At every opportunity, Colonel Ba drummed away at the point that conditions at the camp were much better than enemy propaganda had predicted: he did not poison them; he did not beat up pregnant women; soon he would give everyone food.

A reporter asked him how the present program of "resettlement" differed from the earlier "strategic-hamlet" program, which both Americans and Vietnamese regard as a failure.

"In the strategic hamlet, we could not stay with the people," he answered. "We would leave and the Vietcong would come again. Now we have the Revolutionary Development workers to win their hearts and minds, and teach them about the government. This time we will stay with the people. We can educate them."

In the camp itself, the educational program was represented by the sound truck and the public-address system, the two of which often broadcast propaganda simultaneously. Along with patriotic songs and speeches, announcements were repeatedly played on tape. The following announcement played for about an hour one afternoon: "The 32nd Tactical Area Division and Binh Duong Province welcome you and promise to help you in every way. We know that in the areas under Vietcong control you are terrorized and forced to pay enormous taxes. They promise you everything but never actually do anything good for you. So now the government operation has brought you all here so you can escape from the Vietcong. We are doing our best, but know that food and space are a little short at the moment. In a few days, conditions will improve. The government will soon find a new job for everyone. The Army would like to warn you against the presence of scheming Vietcong cadres in your midst who disguise themselves as refugees. When you see such cadres, come immediately to tell the government troops. We hope that you will be able to go home soon. We also want to request Vietcong cadres to turn themselves in. They will be made welcome in the Open Arms program of the government. This is the only refugee camp in Binh Duong, and we advise all families with relatives still hiding in Ben Suc or in the other towns to come with the Army and try to persuade their relatives over the loudspeakers to come back. The government will always stay with its people!" Propaganda signs were also posted at various points around the camp. One sign, painted on cloth that was draped over the barbed-wire coils at the entrance to the camp, announced in large letters, "WELCOME TO FREEDOM AND DEMOCRACY." A sign farther in, also hanging on the barbed wire, read, "WELCOME TO THE RECEPTION CENTER FOR REFUGEES FLEEING COMMUNISM."

Presently, an N.B.C. reporter asked Colonel Ba where the villagers would be moved for permanent resettlement, and when they would leave the Phu Loi camp.

"We are not sure where they will go yet. They will go to another province in about two months, I think," he answered.

The reporter asked what military operations had been launched in Binh Duong before Operation Cedar Falls.

"Before?" asked Colonel Ba.

"Yes—last year, or the year before."

"Last year?" Colonel Ba slapped his knee and laughed his abrupt laugh. "*I* don't know about last year. I wasn't here." He pointed to himself with both hands in a gesture that cleared him of all responsibility for what had happened last year. "Ask someone else about last year!" he said, dissolving in merriment.

The reporter pursued the matter of a permanent-resettlement area with Colonel White. "Tell me, Colonel, in the new area, will these people be working at the same occupations as they did before?"

"Yes, they will. They will be able to farm just as before. We are giving each family a compensation of five thousand piastres [about thirty-eight dollars]."

"Most of these people are rice farmers. Could you tell me about some of the problems of getting a paddy going? I understand that there are a lot of difficulties at the beginning."

"Yes, we are aware of this, and plan to do everything that's necessary for that," Colonel White answered. As an afterthought, he added, "Maybe they'll grow vegetables."

When the reporter had left the tent, a shadow of perplexity passed over Colonel White's usually cheerful face, and he turned to me and said, "That fellow from N.B.C. didn't look as if he was going to be very nice about what we're doing out here, did he?"

I agreed that he didn't.

Colonel White had a theory about how a reporter might receive an unfavorable impression of the camp.

"I bet that when they talk to the refugees, if they talk to the families *without* men along everyone seems unhappy, but if they happen to talk to families *with* men along everyone seems relatively happy," he said.

A number of American officers assisted Colonel White with matters concerning the camp, but they did not work there full time. Several high-ranking officers, including two generals, made personal tours of inspection in Ben Suc and in the camp. At Phu Loi, the sight of a colonel or a general striding down the aisles between the canopies, followed by staff officers with notebooks, was a common one. I accompanied Colonel John K. Walker, Jr., Senior Adviser to the ARVN 5th Division, on a tour of Ben Suc, and also stayed several days at Gosney Compound, the living quarters of the American Advisory, where I had an opportunity to see what life was like for the Americans after they had finished their day's work at the camp.

Colonel Walker, a tall, forty-eight-year-old man, has a serious, slightly formal air that contrasts with the generally easygoing manner of most of his staff officers, who respectfully refer to him as the Old Man. Living in a room of his own above a dormitory for six staff officers, he often listened to classical music on a tape recorder and, in general, seemed to seek out the company of his fellows less than the other officers did. Sitting in the staff quarters of the compound on the evening before his inspection tour of Ben Suc, I had a chance to talk with him about the war. On the subject of Cedar Falls and the attack on Ben Suc, Colonel Walker said, "What I want to know is: Did you get a feeling of the tremendous firepower we were able to bring to bear, and the precise coördination? The infantryman today has six times the firepower of his Korean counterpart. The troops of the 2nd Brigade were able to land and move to their positions within five minutes. That kind of precision saves American lives. And I'd like to mention that the 2nd Brigade is the finest in the United States Army. You can ask anyone about that. Ask General DePuy about it. And it hurts me to say so, because it's not one of my own. That's what a brigade is—a unit of power. But in this war it's got to be a lot more than that, too. The soldier in Vietnam has to have diverse talents, for dealing with any situation. The military side is only one part. Our men have to fight a war and carry on reconstruction at the same time. This isn't a war for territory, it's a war for the hearts and the minds of the people."

When I asked about the war in general, Colonel Walker said, "This war has many different facets, with the light reflecting in a different way off each of them as it changes. For instance, when we first came here we were losing a lot of men to the V.C.'s night ambushes. Now we're employing his own techniques against him, and a number of V.C. groups have been surprised to find some of our men out there waiting for them when they try to come into a village or move some supplies at night. This is a war with a difference—a weird and beautiful difference. Personally, I feel challenged by it. I'll tell you one thing—it's a heck of a lot more challenging than running a string of gas stations or supermarkets back in the States. But we don't have all the answers yet. The Vietcong is a tough soldier and highly dedicated. When you see people that dedicated, sometimes you wonder: Am I right? Should we be killing them? It gives you pause. But, even with all these problems, the soldier we've got over here today is the best soldier I've seen in three wars. Morale is tops. What I mean by that is that there is less of the kind of complaining from the troops that we used to have in the Second World War and the Korean war. You saw those soldiers helping to unload those trucks for the refugees. They just pitched right in without a word."

The next morning, Colonel Walker flew by helicopter to Ben Suc. The center of the town was empty of villagers now, but some women and children remained in their houses, waiting for boats that would take them down the river to Phu Cuong. A crew of ten-year-old Vietnamese buffalo boys had been helicoptered into the village to round up a herd of buffaloes and take them to boats on the Saigon River. But, aside from these few people and the animals, Ben Suc was now populated by ARVN soldiers. After talking with an American captain about the ARVN search operations in the village, Colonel Walker ordered a jeep in which to drive out from the center of the village along a narrow road. Six

Americans piled onto the jeep, each of them holding a submachine gun. After about five minutes, Colonel Walker stopped the jeep at a clearing on the edge of the woods, jumped out, and strode over to a place where a patch disappeared into a gully. He peered into the undergrowth and suggested that the path was probably used by the enemy. Then, leaving the jeep in the clearing, he struck out across country into the vegetable fields and back yards at the head of a small column of Americans, apparently unconcerned about the danger of land mines, which the Front often plants in such areas. Earlier, one of his staff officers had told me, "An inspection tour with Colonel Walker is quite an experience. He always wants to go right into the brush himself." Coming to a village house, he found that half a dozen ARVN soldiers had moved right in and were enjoying a dinner of the original resident's rice, cooked in his kitchenware and on his hearth. Chicken bones were strewn on the floor and heaped in bowls on a table. Colonel Walker registered a complaint with the soldiers' headquarters over a field radio. Walking back to his helicopter through sunny back yards and copses of palm trees, he told the pilot that he wanted to have a look at the camp at Phu Loi. The pilot flew over the Saigon River at twenty-five hundred feet, and when we neared the camp he circled it twice, coming down to an altitude of five hundred feet. At first, as we wheeled down over the camp, only the red-and-white canopies were visible, but at five hundred feet individual people could be dimly distinguished. The helicopter continued to the ARVN 5th Division landing pad. Helicopters, with their ability to move slow or fast, to circle, and to hover, enabling a viewer to scrutinize a landscape from the top or from any angle, give him a feeling of mastery over a scene, for it seems to him that he has examined it thoroughly, almost scientifically.

At Gosney Compound, I met Major Wade Hampton, who was a member of Colonel Walker's staff and worked full time at the camp. A slender, mild-mannered, courteous man in his mid-thirties, with a strong Southern accent, he told me he usually got up at about six-thirty, to give himself time to eat a leisurely breakfast and finish up his business around the base before leaving for the camp, at about eight-thirty. On his own initiative, I gathered, he had moved his post of operations from an office on the base to a tent at the camp. He came back to Gosney at lunchtime, to eat in the dining hall, and again early in the evening, in time for a hot shower and dinner. Perhaps the most important of his several duties at the camp was to organize and coördinate the dropping of leaflets over the area covered by the Cedar Falls operation. The leaflets, dropped by the tens of thousands, were mainly of two kinds, the Major explained, and he handed me a sample of each. One shows a happy family eating a meal in a cozy grass-roofed house, with their dog sitting outside, near a pretty young girl who stands leaning against a shady tree with her arms folded behind her back, looking sad. The message on the other side reads:

To Our Friends the Cadremen Who Are Still in the War of Liberation for the South

At present, your parents, your wives, your children, and your brothers and sisters who were living in Ben Suc have taken refuge in the township of Binh Duong in order to avoid the exploitation and the suppression of the Vietcong.

Your families have been supplied by the Army and the government of the Republic of Vietnam with money, rice, and decent places for living. Besides all of this, their health is being taken care of by doctors, who give them all kinds of medicine every day. Thus, friends, do not hide in the desolated villages and hamlets anymore and die unreasonably by bullets and bombs.

Come back to the republican regime and live happily and peacefully with your families in this coming spring. How can you forsake your families and let them live in loneliness? The government and the Army are always ready to welcome you back, so that we can build a strong and rich nation together.

With friendly greetings to you all,

The Commanding Headquarters of the 32nd Strategic Area

The second leaflet shows an ARVN soldier, carrying the government flag, mounted on a rearing white horse that has just trampled a tattered flag of the Front on the ground. A tall white cloud rises up behind him. The text reads:

DEAR INHABITANTS
OF THE NHON TRACH AREA

For a long time the Vietcong have threatened your lives, forced you to pay taxes and supply them with rice so that they can lengthen this painful war. They destroy roads and bridges and hinder you in your work.

The Army of the Republic of Vietnam has come here to help you destroy them. So come to your senses and listen to the notices and give the Army and the regime a hand in destroying the Cong and pacifying the people.

You must boldly expose the Vietcong elements who are sneaking into your villages and hamlets to threaten and capture you.

The Army is decisively destroying the barbaric Vietcong with your coöperation, looking forward to the day when peace comes back to your villages.

THE ARMY PROTECTS ITS PEOPLE SO THAT THEY CAN REAP THEIR RICE AND TAKE IT BACK TO THEIR VILLAGES

*The People's Hearts Offensive 81*

Major Hampton explained that Operation Cedar Falls was expected to be particularly effective because "this time we've got their families, and if you've ever been separated from your family like that, you know that it's pure hell—and family ties are particularly strong here in Vietnam, which explains why we've had so many *hoi chanh.*" Oh his bureau Major Hampton had a picture of his wife and children.

I asked why he thought it had been necessary to destroy the villages and evacuate the villagers.

He, in turn, asked if I recalled the villages along the northern edge of the Triangle, and went on, "Tell me, what was the most striking feature of those villages? To me, it was that those people were virtually living underground. It was like a military fortification up there, with bunkers and pillboxes. It looked like the Maginot Line. There was nothing aboveground but a few sticks holding up grass mats."

I suggested that most of the underground rooms might have been used principally for protection against bombs, and not as fortifications.

"I don't think so," he said. "But, at any rate, that was a life of fear they lived. Fear of the Vietcong, fear of the bombs. That wasn't a natural life at all."

Major Hampton had an unusually relaxed and friendly relationship with the men and women who worked for him in his office. He had high praise for one young Vietnamese who prepared translations for him, but sometimes he criticized the Vietnamese, too. Once, when a young woman in the ARVN women's corps told him that she intended to take the customary two-hour midday siesta, he said, in a kidding tone, "That's why you lose the war, Co Ninh, that's why you lose the war."

I mentioned to him that since I had been in Vietnam I had heard almost nothing but criticism and complaints against ARVN troops from the Americans who worked with them. (For instance, one captain who advised ARVN troops told me, "I just can't take it any longer. You can't get anything done with these Arvins, and I'm going out of my mind. I've applied for reassignment to work with our own men again." And when I asked a sergeant who worked under Major Hampton what he thought of the Vietnamese, his reply was "I've worked, eaten, and slept with those villagers for six months, and I want to tell you I have no sympathy for those people. I really don't." One sergeant in the Gosney mess hall, when I asked him whether civilians weren't occasionally killed in the bombings, answered, with a laugh, "What does it matter? They're all Vietnamese.")

Replying to my comment, Major Hampton said, "Speaking for myself, I have great admiration for many Vietnamese. Some of the people I work with are just tops. To me, many of the villagers have a quiet dignity that's extremely impressive. I remember visiting the house of a village elder once. He immediately offered me the greatest hospitality, bringing me a cool drink and inviting me to sit down with his family in their house. We're not supposed to drink unpurified water around here, but I couldn't refuse that drink, although I didn't know what I might get from it."

I told Major Hampton about the cyclist I had seen shot during the attack on Ben Suc, and he said, "When I was out in the field once, a suspect made a break from a group I was guarding. I could have dropped him like that. But I just couldn't do it. I couldn't shoot him like that. So I ran around in front of him and headed him off, and he was recaptured."

Gosney Compound is about five hundred yards up the road from the Phu Loi camp, on one edge of the ARVN 5th Division's base, from which it is separated by a barbed-wire barrier. To enter the compound, one has to pass through a guarded gate. No Vietnamese are permitted to enter on anything but emergency business after 10 P.M. Gosney has much the appearance of an extremely simple but well-kept motel on an American highway. Rows of small white clapboard dormitories for the enlisted men, with neat strips of lawn in front, are grouped across from two larger clapboard buildings, which contain the dining hall and the officers' quarters. The American flag flies from a pole in front of the officers' quarters. Gosney has three clubs, equipped with bars, pinball machines, slot machines for nickels, dimes, and quarters, and a pool table. The smallest club is for the enlisted men, the middle-sized one is for the noncommissioned officers, and the largest—the one with the pool table—is for the commissioned officers. ARVN soldiers serve as bartenders in the enlisted men's and the noncommissioned officers' clubs, but an attractive Vietnamese girl in a gauzy light-purple dress serves the drinks in the club for the commissioned officers. After a hot, dusty day, the men return for a fully American meal, cooked and served by Vietnamese, and perhaps a beer or two, at fifteen cents a can, in one of the clubs. Because it is highly dangerous to go out after dark, and there is nowhere to go anyway, a different movie is shown in the compound almost every night. One night when I was there, they showed "Beau Geste."

On some evenings when war films are shown and the ARVN 5th Division's big guns begin to fire their nightly rounds into the Free Strike Zones, there is momentary confusion in the audience over whether the booming is the Vietnam war outside or, say, "Beau Geste's" Arab-French war in the Sahara. Sometimes the men in Gosney Compound become spectators of the real war, too. Although the compound has never been hit, mortar barrages once landed only a few hundred yards away, and night skirmishes often erupt nearby. On one evening during my visit, as the officers sat out on the porch in front of their quarters sipping soft drinks and criticizing a science-fiction film they had just seen, the slowly moving red lights that indicate helicopters rose into view not more than half a mile away. After drifting back and forth over the treetops for a few minutes, one of the helicopters, apparently finding a target, opened fire with both of its machine guns, directing their aim by red tracer bullets. At first, the fire was wildly diffused, but then the flecks of red from the left side straightened out into a single wavering line of light as the helicopter bore down on the target. The gun on the right continued to send its fire wildly into the landscape immediately below it. Colonel Walker remarked, "The gunner on the left has got his aim all right, but the guy on the right is just spraying those villages over there." The men on the porch could hear the machine-gun fire only as a faint chattering, but after a minute or so there was a series of loud swishes and thumps as the helicopters fired some fifteen rockets at their target. One man on the porch remarked, "If we kill seven of those slant-eyed little bastards tonight, it'll cost the American taxpayer five grand apiece."

For the Americans living in Gosney Compound and working at the Phu Loi camp, the camp created an unpleasant strain, requiring them to work longer hours than usual, but it did not disrupt the basic framework of three solid American meals a day and a movie at night. Although life at the compound was extremely limited and rapidly grew tedious, the wholly American atmosphere, the familiar food, the strong hot showers, and the movies blotted out—for a few hours, at least—the war, the camp, the tension, and the perpetual sense of danger. Once the men had returned to the compound, showered, and put on fresh clothes, they liked nothing less than to have to go out again. On the evening of the villagers' arrival in Phu Loi—when the camp had yet to be constructed and the people were still sitting out in the field—Major Hampton decided that he should go down to the area to see how things were progressing. Stepping out on the porch where his fellow-officers were sitting, he said, "I'm going down to the refugee camp. Does anyone want to come along?"

The men on the porch laughed, and one said, "Are you kidding us, Wade?"

"No. I think we should go down and have a look."

"You're pulling my leg, Wade. Go out? Now? At night?"

Major Hampton went alone.

There is one diversion available outside the compound. Right next to the ARVN dependents' barracks, and about two hundred yards from the Phu Loi camp, the road is suddenly crowded on both sides for about a hundred yards with unpainted, and often freshly constructed, two-story buildings bearing signs, all in English, that read, "Hollywood," "Tokyo," "The Fanny Bar," "Hong Kong," "Happiness Bar," "Snack Bar Sexy," "Scientific Health Massage," and the like. These are bar-brothels, about thirty of which sprang up in immediate response to the buildup of American troops in the area, particularly after the arrival of the 1st Division nearby. A drink for oneself costs about fifty cents, and a drink for one of the "hostesses" costs twice as much. The hostess herself, if she is a prostitute, as about half of the girls are, costs from three hundred to seven hundred piastres (from about two dollars and a quarter to six dollars and a quarter). One of the 1st Division's Military Police told me that his superiors were preventing radical inflation of the prostitutes' fees by the simple expedient of placing establishments off limits—or threatening to—if they got too expensive. If the threat were carried out, it would cut off business completely, for the clientele is entirely American. If the ARVN soldiers should be inclined to go, their base salary of the equivalent of sixteen dollars a month would prohibit it. The strip at Phu Loi is modelled precisely on the original bar district for American servicemen in Saigon, except that what goes on in Saigon at night takes place in sweltering broad daylight—from noon until 5 P.M.—in the rural setting of Phu Loi. The strip is obliged to operate during these peculiar hours because in Phu Loi it is unsafe for an American soldier to venture out after dark. The night still belongs to the enemy. Phu Loi is a small village, and there are as many bars in it as there are all other shops put together. The hot, dusty afternoons at Phu Loi are dominated by the nightlike scenes of the bars. Vietnamese girls from their early teens on up, garbed in low-cut high-hemmed, tight-fitting imitations of evening gowns, wearing Western hair styles, neon-bright lipstick, and heavy eye shadow, stand in the doorways of the bars, in the thick dust from the constant flow of military traffic. Girls just beginning the trade are often shy and wear no makeup, but the ones who are more accustomed to the ways of business on the strip grab at the American soldiers as they pass by in small groups, often carrying opened cans of beer. If the soldiers don't come in, some of the girls taunt them with their few English phrases: "Hey, you cheap Charlie," or "You Number Ten" (the opposite of the phrase for approval, "You Number One"). Among these hostesses, there are occasionally

109

faces of piercing beauty. Mingling with the soldiers out for amusement are soldiers on errands of business, who are distinguishable by the rifles they carry. Most American soldiers carry rifles or submachine guns everywhere they are allowed to, and few Americans appeared at the Phu Loi camp without guns on their shoulders. Carrying a gun becomes second nature, like wearing a watch. A soldier who was about to leave the Gosney Compound for his "r. and r."—rest and relaxation—told me that he felt naked without his gun. Also attracted by the unprecedented flow of money from American hands are beggars of all kinds. They have collected in large numbers at Phu Loi, and, like the bars, they display signs in English. One boy about twelve years old leads his blind mother back and forth in front of the bars on a string, with an English-language sign around his neck asking for money. He is an aggressive beggar and directly confronts soldiers as they step out of the bars onto the dirt road. His mother murmurs something in Vietnamese and bows when her son receives money. At the five-o'clock closing hour, the soldiers all emerge from the bars, often arm in arm with girls and occasionally embracing them on the street. Five o'clock, however, is not the end of the working day for the girls. With imitation-fur stoles over their shoulders and bandannas over their hairdos, they crowd onto a small, dirty blue-and-white bus with a number of other local people and make the bumpy hour-long journey to Saigon, where they go to work again, in the city bars. Most of the Ben Suc villagers in the camp at Phu Loi were not allowed to leave the camp, but on several afternoons groups of women were escorted by ARVN guards to the Phu Loi strip to buy or sell things at the stores that were tucked in between the bars.

On the second and third days of the camp's existence, Lieutenant An's men continued to erect canopies at a feverish rate, and they completed sixty-eight of them before the nylon roofing ran out. Six or seven hundred villagers were still without shelter, and to accommodate them the U.S. 1st Division set up a hundred and fifty hexagonal Army tents about ten feet in diameter and assigned one family to each. The villagers living in these tents stayed outside them in the daytime, because it was impossible to stand up inside except at the very center and the heat under the canvas was suffocating. During the first two days, ARVN soldiers distributed a ration of rice in the camp. The Americans actually supplied the ration, in AID bags printed with a design of two hands clasped in front of a red-white-and-blue shield, but they insisted that the ARVN soldiers distribute the rice to the people. Colonel White said, "We've got to teach them to do this themselves. We could go ahead and hand it out, but we're not here to sell ourselves." When the ARVN soldiers brought the first bags of rice into the camp, at lunchtime on the day after the first canopies went up, women, children, and old people crowded four-deep around them, stretching

out containers of all sizes to be filled. A certain allotment had been planned for each family, but the ARVN
soldiers were unable to tell who belonged to what
family, so were apt to give each person a whole family
allotment, and the rice was exhausted in ten minutes,
leaving a crowd of disappointed women still thrusting
out their pots. Some complained that their families had
not eaten in two days. This scene was repeated in the
evening.

On the third day, a group of fifty Revolutionary
Development workers arrived from Saigon. On the example of the cadres of the National Liberation Front,
most of them were between the ages of eighteen and
twenty-five and wore the simple black peasant garment
first adopted by the Front cadres. At the camp, they
went about their work silently, speaking little to anyone, and leaving the propaganda entirely up to the
loudspeakers, which broadcast ceaselessly thirteen or
fourteen hours a day. (The Psychological Warfare
Office measures its achievements in part by the number
of hours of propaganda played. Thus, in a report on a
so-called New Life Hamlet program carried out at the
southern tip of the Triangle in the last months of 1966,
among such items as "5,269 Medcap patients," "2,200
liters of chemical used for defoliation," "250 acres
cleared by bulldozer for security," and "20,860 sheets of
roofing issued to 1,156 families" are the achievements
"524 hours of Psywar by loudspeaker" and "4 music
concerts conducted.") In sharp contrast to the noisy,

playful ARVN soldiers and their flamboyant officers, the Revolutionary Development workers usually gave no indication of their mood. Like the villagers' withdrawal from contact with anyone around them during the period of the attack and evacuation, the R.D. workers' posture of attending exclusively to their own business and generally drawing as little attention to themselves as possible was very noticeable among a frequently demonstrative, theatrical, hot-blooded people such as the Vietnamese. On those occasions when the R.D. workers did speak to the villagers, the exchanges were extremely short, both sides appearing relieved at being able to terminate the contact quickly. The R.D. workers' first job at the camp was to coöperate with the Province Police in registering, fingerprinting, and photographing the villagers. To solve the problem of food distribution, they issued each registered family a green tag as a ration ticket, which would be marked each time the family received rice.

When I asked to speak to the leader of the R.D. workers, I was introduced to Tran Ngoc Chang, a slight young man who stared off to one side of me as he delivered brief, factual answers to my questions in a soft, deliberate voice, as though he were reciting. He said that his workers slept inside the camp and received a salary of three thousand two hundred and fifty piastres a month (about twenty-four dollars). As leader, he received fifty-two hundred piastres a month (about thirty-nine dollars). When I inquired whether he had any problems with his job at the camp, he answered that he was afraid his crew of only fifty would not be able to handle effectively the needs of the six thousand people who were totally dependent on them. When I inquired about the satisfactions and drawbacks of his job, he answered quickly, "I like to work, and I want to enable the people to realize their aspirations and fulfill their hopes for a new life." I asked for an example of what he meant, and, after a pause for thought, he replied, "For instance, if the people want water, I can get it." Concerning the people's needs at the camp, he said that the most frequent demands were for more food, for permission to leave the camp to relieve themselves, and for permission to return to their villages for more of their possessions. One day, he said, a truckload of women had been taken back to a village that had not yet been destroyed, to fetch their belongings. However, permission to leave the camp for any reason could be granted only by the military, who were very reluctant to let anyone out, so the R.D. workers could not be of much help to the people in this respect.

That day, the ARVN troops began the construction of another latrine, of a more permanent type, which would hide the users from public view. A short time later, a team of Americans with a derrick entered the camp to dig a well. To the desperately bored children, the derrick was a focus of attention. So were sections of piping four feet in diameter strewn around on the ground near it; the children made use of them as a playground, crawling through the sections that were lying on the ground and climbing into the sections standing on end. Also on the third day, water buffaloes and cows began to arrive, in trucks, and were placed in a fenced-off section of the field. On the fourth day, a hundred of the men from Ben Suc were released by the Province Police to join their families in the camp. Just outside the barbed wire near the command tent, the 1st Division set up a mess tent that served hot dogs, chicken, potatoes, Spam, and Keen to the American and Vietnamese soldiers. The wind nearly always blew from the tent toward the camp, and the smell of the cooking wafted down among the villagers, bringing out small crowds of children to stand at the edge of the barbed wire and watch the soldiers receive their dinner on paper plates.

Throughout the first week, work teams from South Vietnam's profusion of patriotic groups for "nation building" arrived at the camp, wearing a wide variety of uniforms. The first to come were five locally recruited girls in their late teens and early twenties, at least three of them strikingly beautiful, who wore conical straw hats and long, flowing, spotlessly white *ao dai*— the traditional women's dress in Vietnam, which consists of wide, ballooning trousers under a long dresslike garment split up the sides to the waist. The girls' job was to help the medical teams by searching through the camp for those in need of medical attention. They were doing this kind of work for the first time and were afraid to approach the villagers directly. For the most part, these young girls—shy, beautiful, and useless— simply clung tightly to their clipboards and kept their eyes trained properly on the air in front of them as they bravely sailed down the dusty aisles between the rows of squatting villagers, like lovely angels in white robes who had been dropped into the camp by mistake. Next to arrive was a wholly different type of girl—a troop of ARVN women, who were clad in tight-fitting Army-green trousers, jackets covered with pockets, and small, high-heeled black leather boots. Many wore sunglasses and sported broad-brimmed green hats of a sort that have lately become very popular among the Vietnamese military. Wholly preoccupied with chattering to each other in low, nervous voices as they made their first appearance, they seemed ready, as a group, to giggle at the entire universe. When I asked a little knot of four of them, through an interpreter, what their job at the camp would be, they all broke into giggles and looked desperately at each other for someone to answer me. Finally, one girl replied, "We don't know yet. We're here to help the refugees." The giggling that followed precluded any further conversation. It seemed to me that every time I walked by the mess tent there was a line of them waiting, paper plates in hand, for hot dogs and Keen. Later, reading a report put out by the American Advisers in the 32nd Division Tactical Area, which described "the relocation of civilians" as "an outstanding success," I read that the ARVN women, who were referred to as "social workers," were "assisting in the necessary administration required in processing the refugees and giving adult hygiene and sanitation classes," and also "taking care of children and looking after anyone requiring medical care."

The villagers themselves began to improvise improvements for their quarters. ARVN soldiers having laid out bamboo poles for them, they split these into long strips, which they lashed together to construct flat panels that could become raised platforms when they were rested on rows of notched bamboo poles driven into the ground. Rudimentary partitions, made of mats, rice bags, and bedclothes, also appeared. After a week in the camp, the children began to show signs of a universally lamented transformation that seems to occur inevitably whenever Vietnamese children are brought into frequent contact with Americans. At first, the G.I.s, charmed by the shyness and reserve of the Vietnamese children and wanting to be friendly, offer pieces of candy or gum. Perhaps the children accept and politely offer thanks, but the next time there is less hesitation, and after several times the children, far from hesitating, demand the handouts. Walking along the road to the camp, for instance, a soldier would often be virtually attacked by groups of children from the ARVN dependents' area. They ran at him screaming, "O.K.! O.K.! O.K.! O.K.!" and turning smiles full of excitement and anticipation up to him as they grabbed both his hands and rifled his pockets. When turned down, they called out, "Cheap Charlie!" with terrible disappointment. The Americans, finding themselves in the unpleasant position of having constantly to refuse candy to smiling children, soon tired of this game. Inside the camp, the children were not yet attacking the Americans, but they had already learned to hold out their hands and shout, "O.K.!" Another more or less inevitable development was the hasty construction just outside the camp, by local Vietnamese, of a whole row of little stands selling beer and soft drinks to Vietnamese at high prices and to Americans at exorbitant prices. When an American objected to paying seventy-five piastres (about fifty-five cents) for a soft drink, the venders, like the prostitutes, the beggars, and the children when they met resistance, would call out, "Cheap Charlie!" and "You Number Ten!"

After most of the villagers had been evacuated from the Triangle, I drove a mile down the road from the camp to the Open Arms center. An armed Vietnamese guard let me pass without identification through a gate. Surrounded by high barbed-wire fences, heavy sandbagging, bunkers, and sentry posts, the Open Arms center consisted of a dirt yard in which several tents had been pitched opposite a long building containing a small café, a room with administrative desks, two interrogation rooms, and a dormitory filled with double-decker beds for the returnees. The interrogators kept one or two returnees busy, propaganda sessions occupied a group in the morning and the early afternoon, and construction work on a small wooden house that was to be a recreation center occasionally occupied another group, but the majority of the returnees spent most of their time asleep, or simply lying on their bunks in the heat. One group of twenty or thirty stood or crouched in a circle, absorbed in a game of cards. Five or six lay stretched out asleep on the board floor of an open-sided Army tent. Some sat around in small groups smoking and talking. (Upon arriving, each man had been issued a package of Cambodian cigarettes and a toothbrush.) All these men were listed in official reports as "Vietcong defectors," but the majority of the returnees from Ben Suc, evidently not yet realizing they were defectors, rather than just prisoners given a special amnesty, claimed that they had never participated as soldiers in the National Liberation Front or coöperated with the enemy in any way, though most said they had paid taxes. They seemed to have been unaware at the moment of their capture that they were "defecting." One returnee, after telling me that he was married and the father of two, went on, in a soft voice, "When the bombs started falling and the helicopters came, I ran into a bomb shelter under my house with my wife and children. Later, the government troops came to the mouth of the tunnel with a loudspeaker and told us to turn ourselves in or be shot. We were scared of being shot! We turned ourselves in and handed the Americans leaflets. Then I was brought here by helicopter. They tell me my wife and children are in a camp nearby."

One American officer concerned with classification problems said, "We aren't going to accept them as *hoi chanh* if they don't turn themselves in until we come along and tell them we're going to blow up their hole and *then* they come running out waving their leaflet."

A seventeen-year-old returnee with his toothbrush sticking up out of his shirt pocket said simply, "When the troops came and the artillery started firing, I hid in the fields. Later, I heard the helicopter announcement. Then I turned in a leaflet I had found a month ago."

Another man, who admitted he had led a squad of five soldiers, said, "When the helicopter came, I ran around from place to place trying to escape, but I couldn't, so I turned myself in to a unit of government troops with a leaflet I had picked up."

In a situation where everyone, whether a defector or not, had to give himself up or be shot, possession of one of the safe-conduct passes dropped at the beginning of the attack had apparently been the key factor in determining who was to be placed in the category of "defector." Generally, the returnees' conversion to the government cause seemed to have involved a minimum of initiative on their part. According to a United States Army report, there were five hundred and twenty-nine returnees in Binh Duong Province in the month of January. In the two neighboring provinces of Phuoc

Long and Binh Long, where no large operations took place, there were only four returnees all told in the same period.

Before leaving the Open Arms center, I sat down for a minute in an open Army tent, whereupon ten or fifteen returnees came over to look at me with sleepy curiosity. Through my interpreter, I asked again about life in Ben Suc, and a young man began to tell me about the bombing of the center of the village and about the government flag they had posted on the rice-storage building to protect the village. I noticed that he was glancing at the other returnees as often as at me, and that he was warming to his story with the relish of a man telling a favorite anecdote to an appreciative audience. Like any good storyteller, he allowed only a twinkle of amusement to appear on his own face, but the other returnees were plainly having a hard time controlling their laughter. Their deadpans were cracking, and I felt that the whole group was suddenly coming to life. "The government told us that if we flew the government flag on any building it would not be bombed," he said, as though he had innocently placed his whole trust in the government. "So we bought a government flag in Phu Cuong and put it on top of the rice-storage building—a big flag it was." He stretched his arms to show his audience just how big. "But then the planes came and they bombed it anyway, and the government flag went down in the bombed building." By this time, several young men in the group had burst out laughing, although most of them were not from Ben Suc. It was a full minute before they resumed their dull, sleepy stares.

During the Phu Loi camp's first week, I spent several afternoons there interviewing villagers from Ben Suc through an interpreter. Before I asked them any questions, I would say that I was a reporter, not connected with the Army. They clearly disbelieved me. At first, they would nod understandingly, but later they would ask me for salt, cooking oil, or rice, or for permission to leave the camp, and I would have to explain again that I had no authority in these matters. They would nevertheless ask several more times for food or privileges, as though my claim to be a journalist were part of a game they had played with many interrogators before me. They refused to believe that this young man—the latest in a long procession of young men, of many political colorations, in their lives—did not want to persuade them of something or use them for his own ends. As we spoke, it was difficult to hear each other above the din of loud, enthusiastic taped voices coming over the public-address system.

When I ducked, with an interpreter, into a section of one canopy and asked a young man who was holding the hand of his three-year-old son if we could talk with him for a minute, he leaned down, smiled at the boy, and told him to go to his mother, a young woman with a broad, open face and large, dark eyes, who was standing nearby. The young man came forward to meet us with an unruffled composure that I encountered again and again in the Ben Suc villagers, as though nothing in the world could be more natural for them than to have a talk with an American. He stood before us with a faint smile of amusement. After introducing myself in my usual way, I asked what he thought about coming to the camp. Through the interpreter he said, "I realize now that there is a war going on and that I have to leave to be defended by the government troops and the Americans. Here it is safe—there will be no bombs and artillery. The crops in my field have all been destroyed by chemicals, and my elder brother was killed by a bomb. Many people were killed when the center of the village was bombed last year. Here we are protected by the American troops."

I asked him what he had enjoyed most in his life at Ben Suc.

With a laugh at being asked such a question, he answered, "I play the guitar, and I liked to sing at night and drink with friends—to eat fish and drink until the sun came up. I am thirty-one now, and was married when I was twenty-three. I have three children. I believe in Confucius and pray to Confucius to keep me from misfortune, to send me good luck, and for peace. On most days, I would get up at six o'clock, eat, have a bath, and then go out to the fields. At midday, I would come back, have another bath, and eat, and I would have a bath again when I stopped working at night. I haven't had a bath in four days now. Do you think we'll be able to have one soon?"

I expressed surprise at his taking so many baths, and told him that most Americans take only one bath a day.

"I don't believe it!" he answered. "We always take three baths a day—four when we are sick. After a bath, you feel healthy and feel like eating a lot. We have become very tired here waiting for food, and for water for a bath."

Outside another canopy, I approached a middle-aged man with long, mussed-up hair who sat cross-legged on a straw mat in front of his compartment, scowling frankly while his wife, squatting next to him, tried to blow life into a small twig fire. It was late afternoon, and a chilly breeze had picked up as the sun moved lower in the sky. The thin, scowling man, who wore only a black shirt and green short pants, was shivering slightly. "I have a stomach ache," he told me, pressing his hands over his belly. "I got here yesterday morning on a boat, but we couldn't bring anything with us. All our things are still in Ben Suc—our oxen, our rice, our oxcarts, our farming tools, and our furniture." He related this without looking at me, in a restrained but disgruntled tone. "Now we have only plain rice to eat—nothing to flavor it, not even salt. They don't bring any food. And there's not enough water to take a bath."

I asked him how he felt about leaving his village.

"Anybody would be sad to leave his village," he said. Then, quoting the loudspeakers, he added, "But we have to be protected by the government and American troops."

At this, his wife turned and said furiously, "We have nothing! I have no cooking oil, no rice! We have to beg from the people next to us!"

I asked her if she knew about the rice distribution by the Revolutionary Development workers.

Now losing all control of her temper, she snatched a green meal ticket out of her pocket and waved it at me. "They gave me a ticket a day ago, but they never have enough rice. We couldn't even bring blankets or clothes. My son is naked. Look!" She pointed to a little naked boy of about four, who stood watching his angry mother. "It's no good for children here. Not good for their health. They get cold at night, and there is nowhere for them to go to play." Abruptly, she turned her back and began trying again to get her fire going.

Her sick husband continued to look at the ground. After a minute or so, he said, "I am actually from Mi Hung, but we moved to Ben Suc six months ago, after Mi Hung was bombed."

I asked how long he thought he would be made to stay in the camp.

"I don't know. I was just put here. I can't do anything about it. I can't speak English. How should I

125

know what they are going to do next? I can't understand what they are saying. Many of the old women were weeping when they were taken away."

At another place, addressing myself to a mother holding a baby, I was immediately surrounded by three mothers. They all wore rolled-up black pants with white or blue shirts—dirty now, since the camp had no washing facilities. At first, only one replied when I asked how they liked life at the camp.

"Everybody was taken away from Ben Suc," she said. "We couldn't bring our rice, and we brought only a few possessions. We ran into the bomb shelters when the bombing started."

When I asked the women about their husbands, they all began talking excitedly:

"My husband was out plowing, but I don't know where he is now."

"We don't know where they are."

"They were taken away."

"I don't know if he is still alive or not."

"I saw people dead in the fields, but I didn't know who they were."

One of the women moved forward, and the others grew silent. "We want to go back, but they are going to destroy everything." She was not supposed to know this yet, but she looked at me evenly as she said it.

I asked her whether she was from Ben Suc.

"I am actually from Yao Tin, and was at Ben Suc only for the harvest, to help my parents. I left all my money and things at Yao Tin. I couldn't even go back to my parents' house after coming to the center of the village. My sister is still at Ben Suc, I think."

Having heard that Vietnamese villages often rely on a group of elders to make decisions on village matters, and thinking that it would be interesting to talk with them, I asked the three women if they could tell me who the village elders of Ben Suc were. As this was translated, a hint of mischievous amusement appeared on the face of one of the women, and with sudden cheerful recklessness she declared, "We didn't have any village elders." Her little smile was contagious, and the three women exchanged conspiratorial glances, like schoolgirls with a secret. Emboldened, the first speaker added, "Nobody was important. Everyone was equal." All three watched my face closely to see how I would react to this gambit.

I asked if anyone had collected taxes.

"No, there were no taxes," another of the women answered. "We used what we grew for ourselves."

The first then said, "There was no government. And no government troops." All three struggled with suppressed amusement.

I asked them how they had liked having no government and no government troops.

At this, they all broke into girlish laughter, hardly even trying to cover their smiles with their hands. No one answered the question. Instead, one of them said, "Anyway, now we must be protected by the government and the American troops." She still could not wholly suppress her rebellious smile. As though to say something calculated to please me even more, she added, "Last year, government troops and Americans came just to give out medicine, and no one was killed."

Another woman said, "This time, many were wounded, killed, or taken away."

In one compartment, an old man sitting on a mat told me, "I was born in Ben Suc, and I have lived there for sixty years. My father was born there also, and so was his father. Now I will have to live here for the rest of my life. But I am a farmer. How can I farm here? What work will I do? There were many killed, but luckily I came safely with my three daughters. They have given us rice here, but I can't eat it. The American rice is for pigs. And we have no cooking oil." (After the first handout of rice, in several places around the camp I noticed pigs with their snouts deep in piles of American rice that had been dumped out by the Vietnamese. Like most East Asians, the Vietnamese are extremely particular about the color, texture, size, and flavor of their rice. Rice also has ritual meanings for them that go beyond matters of taste and nutrition. The Vietnamese welcomed the long-grained, brownish, American-grown rice about the way an American would welcome a plate of dog food—as a dish that was adequately nutritious, and perhaps not even bad-tasting, but psychologically repellent.)

The old man had an idea for his future. "I have

relatives in Phu Cuong who will help me and my daughters. Won't you let me go out of here and build a new house in Phu Cuong, where I can farm?"

Once more I tried to explain that I was not from the government. The old man obviously didn't believe me.

In the morning of the fourth day, there was a high wind, which blew clouds of dust so thick that you couldn't see from one end to the other of the aisles between the canopies. Under one of the canopies, an old man with a wispy goatee and a mild, gracious smile sat on a mat, holding a baby in his arms, in the lee of a pile of possessions and several mats that his family had hung from the bamboo framework to protect themselves from the wind and dust. He smiled down at the baby as it played with a twig. Answering my questions, he said, "I have two sons, but I don't know where they are now. They went into the government Army, and I haven't heard anything about them for several years. Now I live with my daughter." The baby became agitated, beat its arms, and threw away the twig. Shifting the baby into one arm, the old man drew a tobacco pouch from his pocket and gave it to the baby to play with. In the pouch, along with a small box for tobacco and paper for roll-your-own cigarettes, was his newly issued identification card, which already had a slight tear in the center. The baby's interest lit on the I.D. card, and, grasping it tightly in both hands, it widened the tear until the card ripped in two and it was left holding a piece in each hand. The old man, who was delighted with everything the baby did, laughed warmly at its latest deed and smiled at the people around him. Then he put the two pieces back in the pouch and put the pouch in his pocket.

Meanwhile, a little girl who had her hair in a single long, black braid and was wearing golden rings in her ears had approached to watch me, curiosity overcoming fear.

"How old are you?" I asked.

"Eleven."

"What's your name?"

"Ngai."

"What do you do all day?"

"Nothing."

"Nothing at all?"

"I help my mother cook."

"What do you like best here?"

"I like my dog." She hoisted up a black puppy for me to see. "My friend gave it to me."

"What do you like least here?"

"It's too hot and crowded. I like my aunt's house."

"Why?"

"It's cool. It has walls."

The old man laughed in agreement.

As I stood up to leave, I saw that Ngai was wriggling with inner conflict and staring at me with a smile of determination and excitement. Then I saw that she was holding her hand out, palm upward but close to her body, in an irresolute play for a gift of candy from the American, but almost as soon as she had mustered the courage she lost it and turned away from me in embarrassment.

Under another canopy, a woman with a blank, lonely gaze sat holding a tiny baby. She hardly seemed to notice me as I approached her. When I addressed her, she talked as though she were thinking out loud, and didn't answer any questions directly. She said, "The helicopters came early in the morning while I was on my way to the field. My husband is in Saigon now. I think he's in Saigon. The loudspeakers came overhead, but how could I hear them? The bombs were exploding everywhere. My father is deaf, so how could he hear the voices from the helicopter? Now I don't know where he is. All I could bring was my children and my clothes. My father is very old. Maybe he is dead."

The demolition teams arrived in Ben Suc on a clear, warm day after the last boatload of animals had departed down the river for Phu Cuong. G.I.s moved down the narrow lanes and into the sunny, quiet yards of the empty village, pouring gasoline on the grass roofs of the houses and setting them afire with torches. Columns of black smoke boiled up briefly into the blue sky as the dry roofs and walls burned to the ground, exposing little indoor tableaux of charred tables and chairs, broken cups and bowls, an occasional bed, and the ubiquitous bomb shelters. Before the flames had died out in the spindly black frames of the houses, bulldozers came rolling through the copses of palms, up-rooting the trees as they proceeded and lowering their scoops to scrape the packed-mud foundations bare. When the bulldozers hit the heavy walls of the bomb shelters, they whined briefly at a higher pitch but continued to press ahead, unchecked. There were very few dwellings in Ben Suc to make a bulldozer pause. The bulldozers cut their own paths across the back-yard fences, small graveyards, and ridged fields of the village, ignoring the roads and lanes. When the demolition teams withdrew, they had flattened the village, but the original plan for the demolition had not yet run its course. Faithful to the initial design, Air Force jets sent their bombs down on the deserted ruins, scorching again the burned foundations of the houses and pulverizing for a second time the heaps of rubble, in the hope of collapsing tunnels too deep and well hidden for the bulldozers to crush—as though, having once decided to destroy it, we were now bent on annihilating every possible indication that the village of Ben Suc had ever existed.

# OTHER NEW YORK REVIEW CLASSICS

*For a complete list of titles, visit www.nyrb.com.*